BEYOND FINISHING WELL

Writing Life's Next Chapter

With Questions
for Reflections and Discussion

David W. F. Wong

WESTBOW
P R E S S®
A DIVISION OF THOMAS NELSON
& ZONDERVAN

WestBow Press books may be ordered through booksellers or by contacting:

WestBow Press
A Division of Thomas Nelson & Zondervan
1663 Liberty Drive
Bloomington, IN 47403
www.westbowpress.com
1 (866) 928-1240

ISBN: 978-1-4908-6475-4 (sc)
ISBN: 978-1-4908-6476-1 (hc)
ISBN: 978-1-4908-6474-7 (e)

Library of Congress Control Number: 2014922987

Print information available on the last page.

WestBow Press rev. date: 01/12/2016

ENDORSEMENTS

"I first met David Wong nearly 40 years ago when we were both embarking on our ministries—his as a pastor in his home country of Singapore and mine to Indonesia. Now we are both involved in preparing the next generation of Gospel ministers. This book adds to what David has already written on finishing well by presenting stimulating and interesting vignettes of various biblical characters who have either succeeded or failed to hand on their ministry. The biblical work is strengthened by examples from more recent church history.

"David's words in his chapter on Joshua sum up the message of this useful book: 'Succession, left to chance and the forces of nature, will not work. If we do not cherish our faith enough to pass it on, we stand to lose it all by the third generation.'"

Revd. Ray Porter
Director of World Mission Studies
Oak Hill Theological College, London

"David Wong is one of the wisest men I know, and he generously shares his wisdom in this book. David speaks from real-life experience. We had the opportunity to spend many hours, discussing the matter of successful successions. I saw how he literally agonized in his heart, watching failed successions and searching for a better way in the art of succession.

"David is passionate about *Finishing Well* and has taught seminars on that subject on every continent. This book is relevant wherever you are. But what makes it special is that it is Bible-based. David shows how, following biblical principles tested and proven in history, we can avoid the collapse of family business, corporate enterprise and Christian ministry after our generation. This book should be a study guide for all of us. I plan to give it to many friends in different parts of the world. It is a necessary and urgent work!"

Reginaldo Andre Kruklis
Senior Pastor, International Protestant Church, Zurich, Switzerland
Former President, Haggai Institute

"Why beyond? Is finishing well in one's lifetime not enough? Is getting to the finish line not what counts in the end? No, it is not. From Genesis to Revelation God makes it clear that we are responsible to pass on to the next generation what has been entrusted to us. In fact, the biblical accounts testify to the fact that people who finished well have also faithfully engaged in the transmission of their faith and the succession of their leadership. Therefore, *Beyond Finishing Well* is not only a welcome, but an imperative sequel to *Finishing Well.*

"In this sequel, David Wong focuses on the lives of a dozen biblical characters, and presents helpful insights and principles on leadership succession from a biblical perspective. His unique way of story-telling, of asking intriguing questions, of weaving together the study of the Bible with contemporary literature and events, undergirded by his long-standing personal experience in leadership succession, makes the reading of this book captivating. I recommend this book as a tool for personal enrichment and ministerial equipment."

Dr. Marlene Enns
Faculty, Practical Theology, Facultad de Teología
Universidad Evangélica del Paraguay, Paraguay

"David Wong and I had the privilege of serving together on Maui at Waipuna Chapel as well as at the Haggai Institute's Mid-Pacific Center. David's previous book, *Finishing Well: Closing Life's Significant Chapters* was most influential in my life. It helped me and the congregation of our church to complete one season of ministry and successfully transition to the next pastor.

"Now David takes us *Beyond Finishing Well* to *Writing Life's Next Chapter*. As in the first book, he presents compelling biblical characters, brings forward lessons from their lives into today's context, makes us think about the significant issues involved, and presents challenging application possibilities. What more could an intentional follower of Jesus Christ ask for from a book that challenges each reader to live life informed and directed by a truly biblical worldview? I highly recommend this book to you!"

Donn W. Anderson
Mentor and Spiritual Director
Pastor Emeritus, Waipuna Chapel, Maui, Hawaii

"I first met Dr Wong 15 years ago in Maui, and have since then benefitted from the depth of insights from his writing and teaching. He has a unique style of presentation that brings lessons to life for his audience. In *Beyond Finishing Well*, he uses case studies of biblical characters to drive home profound truths and dispense life-changing wisdom from the Word of God. The reader will relate readily to his blend of ancient and contemporary events and examples.

"I recommend Dr Wong's latest book, not only to the global Christian community and its leaders but also to the business world, where the challenges of continuity and succession are real and urgent. "

Peter Ameadaji
Managing Partner, PAC Solicitors, Attorneys at Law
Lay Pastor, Foursquare Gospel Church, Lagos, Nigeria

"David Wong had a great impact on the lives of thousands of leaders when he was the Director of International Training at Haggai Institute in Maui, Hawaii. I have always admired David's revolutionary and creative thinking. In this book, David deals with the sensitive issue of leaders stepping down, paving the way for other leaders to blossom and lead. In a readable style and with clear arguments, David cites examples from the Bible and from real life to illustrate and support his call for succession.

"I strongly commend this book to both church and secular leaders. I believe that the Christian principles contained in this book can help solve many leadership problems in our world."

Dr. Menes Abdul Noor
Pastor Emeritus
Kasr el-Dobara Presbyterian Church, Cairo, Egypt

"Leadership succession is only a nice theory unless it works in practice. Succession involves many components: selecting the candidates, checking their track records, observing them in action—also, convincing the board and the constituency to stand by the successor. All these require a great deal of courage and wisdom.

"In this book *Beyond Finishing Well*, Dr David Wong has interwoven important factors of biblical successions with contemporary examples to be applied to leadership today. I have seen Dr Wong fearlessly and gracefully walk the talk of succession and finishing well in the 40 years of our friendship. His track record and commitment to prepare leaders and pass on responsibilities makes me to vouch that this book is not about nice theories but about actual practice. With confidence and warmth I recommend this book to inspire us towards planning succession and leaving a legacy along the line of 2 Timothy 2:2."

Dr. K. Rajendran
Consultant, Global Roundtables of Innovation
& Leadership Development, Hyderabad, India

"Rev David Wong, who shepherded a church that planted other churches and directed an institute that trained leaders around the world, reflects on leadership: What is a leader? Who is a leader? Whose is the leader? He answers them only to further ask: What goes beyond *finishing well*—beyond accomplishing the assigned task, beyond stepping out unscathed, beyond improving on one's predecessor? It is, he says, effective succession. His well-researched and timeless insights in an area not frequently discussed and often poorly practised are biblically rooted, historically illustrated, and globally relevant."

Rev. Dr. Michael Shen
Professor in Bible Exposition
& Former Principal, Singapore Bible College, Singapore

"*Beyond Finishing Well* is inspiring and convincing. Life is not only about reaching the finish line, but about leaving behind a good legacy to the next generation. Dr David Wong makes profound truths easy to understand. His story-telling touches the heart and offers wisdom for living. Like his earlier work, *Finishing Well*, this is a must-read book!"

Maimunah Natasha
Businesswoman & Entrepreneur
Chairperson, Haggai Institute National Board, Jakarta, Indonesia

"What a joy to have another book from David Wong! His works are always Scriptural, full of insights and inspiration. As translator of *Finishing Well* into Japanese, I saw the earlier book warmly accepted and greatly appreciated. This sequel will help Christian leaders towards a better understanding of God's Word in regard to succession and successful transition which are issues of serious importance to many churches. Readers will find God's wisdom and guidance for themselves and for their ministry."

Daiso Koyama
Pastor, Gifu Full Gospel Church
Vice-Chairman, Kansai Bible Institute, Japan

"I write as the seventh Archbishop of the Anglican Church in Uganda. My predecessors before me went through a great revival known as the 'East African Revival' They were familiar with the spiritual fire that brought convictions to many. In the intervening years, however, this fire had begun to fade. As the leadership grew older, there was a lack of leadership renewal. The work of the Holy Spirit could not go beyond them. The more the leaders held on to leadership, the less influential they became to the next generation. They were out of touch with the needs of the fast changing world.

"Today, thankfully, I see a fresh wind fanning the flame and passion, especially among our young people. In his well-written book David Wong shows the importance of anticipating the future while reflecting on the past. How has God worked among us? How is he still working in our time? What are we passing on to the next generation? David argues the case for smooth succession from older leaders to younger leaders. Both Old Testament and New Testament point to the great need for leaders as they come and go, and as God chooses, prepares and deploys them. My personal interaction with David has left in me a lasting impression of a man whose life speaks his words. I am thankful that this work has come to meet the growing needs of our generation."

The Most Rev. Henry Luke Orombi
Archbishop, Church of the Province of Uganda
Kampala, Uganda

"If you have concerns for the next emerging generation of leaders, the challenges of leadership renewal, or personally, on how to graciously step aside from your leadership role and to finish your life well, this book is for you. Written with deep insights, it calls for serious reflection by all Christian leaders. Leader development and leadership succession are major issues of any church or Christian organization. David Wong looks at these and other relevant leadership issues from his study of Scriptures, with lessons drawn from his vast experience as a pastor and organizational leader.

"The book takes a long-range view of leadership and highlights the importance of handling leadership processes and transitions well. You will discover from each chapter, as I have, new and fresh insights not found in the many books on leadership. As a mentor in intergenerational leadership development, I heartily recommend this book for all leaders."

Jim Chew
Senior Missions Mentor, The Navigators
Wellington, New Zealand

DEDICATION

To my predecessors
Richard Bowie and Quek Swee Hwa
and my successors
Daniel Chua and Aldo Fontao

CONTENTS

Introduction

Why Successions Fail

In the seminars I conduct on *Finishing Well*, I ask the question: "What would you have done, acquired or become, to be able to say, 'I have finished well'"? One common answer is: "If I have passed on my faith to my children." A less common answer is: "If I have passed on my leadership to my successor." Both are equally important. Each expresses our concern for the next generation, whether it be found in our family, our church or our vocation.

Yet, for many of us, parents and leaders, passing on our faith and our leadership does not appear to be a priority, at least not in practice. There are a number of reasons. Firstly, we are too busy taking care of the needs of the present. Parents work hard to provide for their children, and leaders work hard to meet the demands of their constituents. We have no time to think about succession. Even when we do, we consider it something to pursue farther down the road.

Secondly, successful leaders who enjoy what they are doing are seldom serious about succession. They want to continue what they do indefinitely. The thought of retirement appals them. Talk about stepping down sounds to them like a death sentence. Pioneers of enterprises and founders of organisations thrive on challenge and have no intention to slow down. They prefer to die doing what they are doing.

Likewise, leaders of churches and Christian organisations consider it gallant and laudable to serve God till their last breath. However, they confuse serving God with occupying a position. Here lies the third reason why succession is an unwelcome subject. Stepping down from a position is seen as abandoning our post, even betraying our call. The fallacy of such thinking is obvious: serving God is not limited to a position. We can vacate a position and continue serving in a different role, with or without a position.

A fourth reason why we sidestep succession is the insecurity we harbour as leaders. Many of us build our work and ministry around our own insecurity: we feel fulfilled in meeting the needs of the people to the point that we need them more than they need us. No wonder we feel lost and disoriented when we are away from our constituency. But with our own people who recognise and need us, we are at ease and at home. It is hard to step out of that comfort zone.

STEPPING INTO WRONG SHOES

Not only are leaders reluctant to think about succession, they are sometimes the very reason behind failed successions. I have personally witnessed successors being announced, one after the other, by the predecessor, only to see them fall out of favour, one after the other. Each was written off, before he took office or soon after he did so. In one organisation, I saw four failed successions in less than 10 years. It was evident that the incumbents had not helped to make the successions work.

The predecessor may have unrealistic expectations of his successor. The former may say, "I do not expect my successor to wear my shoes." But every successor knows the fine line he walks in navigating his way out his predecessor's shadow. Michael Watkins of Harvard Business School gives a new leader 90 days or three months to settle in and move forward. His description of that period sounds daunting.

"Transitions are periods of opportunity, a chance to start afresh and to make needed changes in an organization. But they are also periods of acute vulnerability, because you lack established working relationships and a detailed understanding of your new role. If you fail to build momentum during your transition, you will face an uphill battle from that point forward."[1]

Vulnerability is the right word, and often a transition runs aground on the rocks of unfair expectations. A successor may be expected to perform beyond his capacity, or conform against his individuality. Such expectations may come, not only from the predecessor, but also from the people. The latter is another reason for aborted successions.

People do not take to change easily. When the slightest discomfort sets in with a new leader, they long to have the old one back. Who can blame them for comparing one with the other? This is especially so when the predecessor has been with them for some time, when strong relationships have been established, and emotional ties forged. How can a successor surmount such odds, coming as they do from his predecessor and the people? No wonder successful successions are such a challenge!

WRITING THE NEXT CHAPTER

Yet, we have no choice but to face the challenge head-on. Finishing well involves closing life's significant chapters. But it does not end with closing a chapter—it goes beyond to writing the next chapter. In 2005, Regent College of Vancouver, Canada, initiated a capital campaign to raise C$15 million to take the school into the new millennium. It carried an appealing tagline, *A story this good…* *deserves another chapter,* and called on supporters to invest in *Writing the Next Chapter.* Is it presumptuous to think we can write life's next chapter? Not really, when we consider how giving now to a project means investing in its future impact.

Similarly, what we do now can influence what happens next. In fact, writing the next chapter is not an option. We are already doing it, whether we know it or not. What we do or fail to do now is affecting the people and events after us. Leaving behind a legacy is not a choice; the question is whether we leave behind a good legacy or a bad one. Paul J. Meyer reminds us:

> "When all is said and done, each of us will leave only four things behind: memories (thoughts that others have of us), souvenirs (proof of our existence), trophies (records of our achievements), and legacies (everything you are and possess today). Eventually, memories will fade and souvenirs and trophies will be lost, stolen, or sold at garage sales. Only our legacy will remain."[2]

What is our legacy to the generation after us? Should we be concerned about it? Of course, we should. Such concern for the succeeding generation is found in the Bible from Genesis to Revelation. How could anyone miss it? When God sets the rainbow in the sky for Noah, he speaks of a covenant for "all future generations."[3] When he introduces himself to Moses, he speaks of himself as "the God of Abraham, the God of Isaac, and the God of Jacob."[4] In one instance, he refers to generations to come; in the other, he refers to generations past. God leaves us in no doubt that he wants us to think beyond one generation. Whether harking back to the past or looking forward to the future, God works across the passage of time.

Across the pages of Scriptures are told stories of a succession of patriarchs and kings, priests and prophets. When we reach the end of the line and meet the apostles, one of them, John, was told to write down what he saw.[5] He did, and the result is the book of Revelation we hold in our hands today. Earlier, John had written a Gospel on the life of Jesus, and ended it with these words, "Now there are also many other things that Jesus did. Were every one of them to be written, I suppose that the world itself could not contain the books that would be written."[6] Though what was written was meant to be read by the readers of his time, as were the epistles by Paul and others, God intended the written records for the generations to come.

As God speaks and works across generations, so he warns us of our influence upon subsequent generations. The sins of the fathers are visited upon their children "to the third and the fourth generation," just as the faith of the fathers reap untold blessings to thousands after them.[7] Paul could look back on the events as far back as the exodus, and claim, "Now these things took place as examples for us... they were written down for our instruction..."[8] How they wrote their subsequent chapters become exemplars or warnings to us on how we should write ours.

As the Regent College's tagline suggests, we do have a good story, and it deserves another chapter—a good one—to follow. This book is all about stories, from the Bible, from history, from contemporary life.

"Story is the most adequate way we have of accounting for our lives, noticing details that turn out to be pivotal, appreciating the subtle accents of color and form and scent that give texture to our actions and feelings, giving coherence to our meetings and relationships in work and family, finding our precise place in the neighbourhood and in history. Story relishes sharp-edged, fresh-minted details; but story also discovers and reveals substrata of meaning and purpose and design implicit in all the details."[9]

The genre of story runs throughout this book. Discussion about legacy and succession makes a cosy pastime for people sitting around on armchairs. But we would rather get into the rough and tumble of real life story, with its feel of blood and the smell of sweat, its taste of tears and the sound of laughter. Ahead of us are twelve or more biblical characters to show us the way.

Finally, though we will speak much of human intrigue and initiatives, chance encounters and fortuitous events, we must not forget the unseen hand of God moving through the generations. In the final analysis, it is the divine hand at work, drafting and writing each chapter of human history.

ACKNOWLEGDEMENTS

I am grateful to the Session of Zion Bishan Bible-Presbyterian Church, Singapore, for granting me a three-month sabbatical to work on this book. During that time, my wife and I enjoyed the hospitality of many friends, in particular when I worked at the libraries of Tyndale House, Cambridge, and of Regent College, Vancouver. Special thanks go to Pauline Koe, Becky Moody, and Leong Weng Chee for their invaluable help with reading the proofs, and to those who shared with me their succession stories. This book could not have been written without the encouragement and prayers of many people. To them I am indebted.

Chapter One

Moses
Must We Do It All Alone?

As a young man, I read a book on spiritual leadership by J. Oswald
Sanders. I was greatly challenged by the examples of leaders he
cited. In a chapter on qualities essential to leadership, he described
what I then aspired to become:

> "The young man of leadership caliber will work while
> others waste time, study while others sleep, pray while
> others play. There will be no place for loose and slovenly
> discipline in diet and deportment, so that he might wage a
> good warfare. He will without reluctance undertake the
> unpleasant task which others avoid, or the hidden duty
> which others evade because it evokes no applause or wins
> no appreciation."[10]

Rightly or wrongly, I understood it to mean I must do what others
do not do, what others do not wish to do, and what others expect me
to do. When I became a pastor, I kept that iconic leader in mind,
putting in long and irregular hours. I felt good when I was busy and
guilty when I was not. Two decades later, disciplined by the rigors of
theological studies and fatigued by the demands of pastoral ministry, I
took a sabbatical. It was then I read a book by Eugene Peterson.

To make a counter-point, Peterson coins a new word as he extols
the *unbusy* pastor. Like many in public service, the pastor is perceived

as busy and praised for being so. But Peterson does not see busyness as a sign of commitment, but rather as a mark of betrayal: "The adjective *busy* set as a modifier of a pastor should sound to our ears like *adulterous* to characterize a wife, or *embezzling* to describe a banker."[11] Strong words indeed, but perceptive and pertinent to the issue of leadership, especially as it applies to succession.

Moses certainly qualified as a busy leader. He "sat to judge the people, and the people stood around Moses from morning till evening."[12] The people had problems and saw Moses as the only one who could help them. Moses cared for the people and felt he was the only one who could attend to them. It took an outsider and an older man, Jethro, to see what was wrong. Moses and his one-man-show did not impress him at all. The people of Israel, watching their leader Moses at work, saw it as an act of consummate dedication. Single-handedly, doggedly, Moses was handling all the people's problems.

But Jethro, like Peterson, saw it differently.

"When Moses' father-in-law saw all that he was doing for the people, he said, 'What is this that you are doing for the people? Why do you sit alone, and all the people stand around you from morning till evening?' And Moses said to his father-in-law, 'Because the people come to me to inquire of God; when they have a dispute, they come to me and I decide between one person and another, and I make them know the statutes of God and his laws.' Moses' father-in-law said to him, 'What you are doing is not good. You and the people with you will certainly wear yourselves out, for the thing is too heavy for you. You are not able to do it alone.'"[13]

DANGER! ONE MAN AT WORK

Jethro saw the situation as untenable and unsustainable. We are all guilty, as leaders and as followers, of creating such a situation in our church or organisation. As leaders, we consider it our duty to do the work. Our heart is right, and our intention is good. So we give ourselves wholly to the work. We not only do the work, we do all the work. Soon we do all the work all the time. Like Moses, we end up as a one-man operation.

The followers are also at fault. They refuse to see anyone else. They clamour for the leader and make him feel like a super-hero, each party contributing to an unhealthy relationship of co-dependency. The leader derives fulfilment from helping the people, and the people derive satisfaction from getting help from the leader. They cannot function without each other. Jethro saw the danger and warned Moses against it.

Firstly, there is the short-term danger. The work exhausts Moses, and in his fatigue, his ability to perform declines, making him liable to mistakes, and err in his judgment. The people also feel the strain. Having to wait a long time to see him, they are tiring themselves, feeling impatient and frustrated. If their problem is urgent, it may already have become worse. According to Jethro, both leader and people are affected.

Secondly, there are the long-term consequences against such a plan of work. No one else will be able to do what Moses is doing. If something happens to him, the people are left without anyone to help them. They have come to depend so much on him—will they know what to do when he is not around? In fact, if Moses continues to do what he is doing, he is likely to kill himself. He may be able to do it when he is younger, but can he continue to do it when he gets older?

So Jethro proposes another plan of work:

"Now obey my voice; I will give you advice, and God be with you! You shall represent the people before God and bring their cases to God, and you shall warn them about the statutes and the laws, and make them know the way in which they must walk and what they must do. Moreover, look for able men from all the people, men who fear God, who are trustworthy and hate a bribe, and place such men over the people as chiefs of thousands, of hundreds, of fifties, and of tens."[14]

Notice how Jethro directs Moses attention away from himself. Instead of doing the work himself, Moses is to teach the people so they will know the way they must walk. Instead of doing the work himself, Moses is to find capable men to do the work with him. So Jethro's two-pronged plan involves teaching the people, and delegating the work to others.

Firstly, leaders should teach the people. Note that teaching is different from telling. It is easier to tell the people what to do than to teach them to do what they should do. Moses should teach the people "the statutes and the laws" to show them the way to walk and the decision to take.

Many years ago, a lady called to ask me for help. She was a nurse in a government hospital and had received an offer to join a private hospital. She was not sure if she should take up the offer. I asked her to list the advantages and disadvantages of working in the public and the private sectors. I then asked her about her preferences and inclinations. After about half an hour, she said, "Pastor, this is really hard for me to decide. You are my pastor. You are a man of God. Surely you know what God's will is for me. Just tell me if I should take the offer—yes or no."

I told her I would not. It was her decision, not mine. My part was to help her arrive at a decision by spelling out certain principles and considering the different factors. I could not decide for her. I wanted her to learn the decision-making process. In the future, when she had to make similar decisions, she would know what to do.

That is *teaching*. We teach our people so they know God's laws and principles, and learn to make decisions for themselves. Of course, if they are not sure, they can consult the pastor or the leader, but in time, they grow in knowledge and maturity, and become less and less dependent on their leaders. In any case, our role as leaders is to not make people dependent on us. It is to help them look to the Lord and be dependent on him. Also, when people are able to take care of themselves, they can also help take care of others. This brings us to the second part of Jethro's wise counsel: select capable men (and women).

MISSING THE GENERATIONS

It is strange that Moses never thought of this. In the preceding chapter, God had already hinted to him that he could not operate alone.[15] As Moses led the people towards Sinai, a tribe known as the Amalekites attacked the Israelites. Moses assigned a young man, Joshua, to lead the fighting men against the attackers.

Moses himself went up a hill to stand with the staff in his hands. He took two other men with him, Aaron his older brother and Hur a younger man. As long as Moses' hands were held up with his staff, Joshua was winning the battle. But when his hands got tired and he let them down, Joshua was losing. So Aaron and Hur stood on either side of him and helped him raise his hands, till Joshua won the victory.

The obvious take-home lesson for Moses was that the battle belonged to the Lord: as long as he held up his hands to the Lord, God gave him the victory. Not so obvious was another lesson. In the battle against the Amalekites, Moses had three men working with him: Joshua, Aaron and Hur. Why did he enlist their help in fighting in a battle, but not in solving the people's problems? In each instance, Moses grew tired holding up his hands all day and listening to problems all day. Surely, God did not intend him to do it alone.

The three men with Moses represented different generations. Joshua eventually took over the leadership from Moses when they reached the Promised Land some 40 years later. He must have been young, probably a generation younger. Aaron was Moses' older brother, not much older, so they belonged to the same generation. Hur is mentioned as the son of Caleb,[16] one of the spies who went to scout the Promised Land. In that mission, Joshua and Caleb were the only two spies who demonstrated faith in God. They were likely to be contemporaries. If so, Hur, would represent the third generation after Moses.

Moses had three generations working together with him. Could God be sending a message to Moses, and could Moses have missed it altogether? So God sent Jethro to make the message clear: Find other leaders, and involve them in the work. Share your work, and pass it down to the younger generations.[17]

Why do some leaders find it hard to share their work with others? On the surface, the reason appears to be a sense of commitment: they want to do a good job, and they feel obliged to get it done themselves. But beneath the surface, there are two unhealthy reasons. One is impatience: it is easier to do it myself than to teach someone else to do it. The other reason is pride: I can do it better, and no one can do it the way I do it.[18]

Such is the essence of the "messiah complex"—the feeling that we are the saviour of the world and we can solve all its problems. People who are task-oriented and multi-talented are most prone to this complex. Unless we recognise our own impatience and pride, we will not delegate. Perhaps, in Moses' case, it was also ignorance. He did not know there was another way—until Jethro told him.

When he heard Jethro's counsel and proposal, he immediately implemented it: "So Moses listened to the voice of his father-in-law and did all that he had said."[19] Jethro's counsel was not just wise human counsel. He made it clear to Moses that it came from God: "If you do this, God will direct you, you will be able to endure, and all this people also will go to their place in peace."[20] Interestingly, God did not speak to Moses directly on this matter as he had done so on other matters, at other times. God chose to speak through Jethro, evidently to underline the point to Moses that he could work through other individuals as well, not just through him.

RESET TO SOLO MODE

Moses implemented Jethro's proposal, but did he learn his lesson? Apparently not. When the people of Israel took leave of Mount Sinai where Jethro had counselled Moses, more pressures piled upon Moses. Previously, the people had come to Moses with their problems; now they accused Moses of *being* the problem. Their diet had been nothing but manna dropped from heaven by God, and though it met their hunger, they were growing tired of it. They longed for meat, together with delicacies like cucumbers, melons, leeks, onions and garlic.[21]As the people complained to Moses, so Moses complained to God: "I am not able to carry all this people alone; the burden is too heavy for me."[22]

Had Moses reverted to his default mode of a "solo" mindset? Note his use of the word *alone*; no wonder he felt the weight of his responsibility. As is often the case, we seldom learn our lesson the first time, and God has to teach us again. As God spoke through Jethro earlier, now God instructed Moses directly:

"Gather for me seventy men of the elders of Israel, whom you know to be the elders of the people and officers over them, and bring them to the tent of meeting, and let them take their stand there with you. And I will come down and talk with you there. And I will take some of the Spirit that is on you and put it on them, and they shall bear the burden of the people with you, so that you may not bear it yourself alone."[23]

God did not intend for Moses to bear the burden of leadership alone. It was Moses who placed the burden solely upon himself. Upon the 70 elders, God put his Spirit so that they would shoulder the responsibility with Moses. Much later, the prophet Joel would announce a similar outpouring of the Spirit: "Even on my servants, both men and women, I will pour out My Spirit in those days." The apostle Peter echoed the prophecy on the Day of Pentecost when the Spirit came upon all the believers gathered.[24]

It is clear that no one leader has the monopoly of the Spirit. He may be the first in line, but there are others after him, and with him. The number of elders reminds us of the 70 whom Jesus appointed to go with the 12 chosen disciples.[25] One of the Jesus' closest disciples, John, wanted to keep the rights and privileges within the inner circle of 12. When he saw someone who was not part of them casting out demons, he asked Jesus to stop him. Jesus refused. The account mirrored the one here where Joshua demanded the same of Moses when two persons who were not present with the elders, started prophesying. Moses too refused.

Moses seemed to have grasped the point that God was making when he replied Joshua, "Are you jealous for my sake? Would that all the LORD's people were prophets, that the LORD would put his Spirit on them!"[26] Moses was learning: he was not the only one with the Spirit. The more individuals the Spirit empowered to serve, the better. In fact, it would be best if *all* of God's people could be thus endowed.

LESS DONE, MORE ACCOMPLISHED

But the final test for Moses was yet to come. As the 40 years of wandering drew to a close, Moses looked forward to taking the people into the Promised Land. He had understood this to be his life's mission ever since he delivered the Israelites out of Egypt. Then God dropped the bombshell: Moses would take the people to the Promised Land, not into it. "Go up into this mountain of Abarim and see the land that I have given to the people of Israel. When you have seen it, you also shall be gathered to your people, as your brother Aaron was...."[27]

God had prepared Moses for this, as the poignant reference to Aaron tells us. Earlier on, Moses had trekked up a mountain with Aaron and Aaron's son Eleazar, and come down with only Eleazar. Aaron's priestly robes had found a successor.[28] The response of Moses shows him ready to accept that he was no longer indispensable:

> "Let the LORD, the God of the spirits of all flesh, appoint a man over the congregation who shall go out before them and come in before them, who shall lead them out and bring them in, that the congregation of the LORD may not be as sheep that have no shepherd."[29]

God answered Moses' request by pointing him to Joshua. As Eleazar succeeded his father Aaron as priest, so Joshua would succeed Moses as leader of the people of Israel. However central and vital a role Moses had played till now, it was time for him to step aside for someone else.

What lessons do we learn from Moses about leadership succession? Firstly, succession begins with a leader who realises his limitations. Late in life, Moses would recount to the people the time when he began delegating his work.

> "At that time I said to you, 'I am not able to bear you by myself. The LORD your God has multiplied you, and behold, you are today as numerous as the stars of heaven.... How can I bear by myself the weight and burden of you and your strife? Choose for your tribes wise, understanding, and experienced men, and I will appoint them as your heads.'"[30]

It took the complaints of the people—both among themselves and against Moses—to tip him over the edge of desperation. When he finally learned he could not do it alone, he also learned he need not do it alone.

Secondly, succession proceeds with a leader who shares his work. When Moses reached the end of his resources, God showed him the resources available in others. It is likely that, at Jethro's advice and also at God's instruction, Joshua was among those selected to serve alongside Moses. Apart from being a military field commander, Joshua accompanied Moses up the mountain to receive the Law, and kept watch over the sacred tent whenever Moses spoke to Yahweh.[31]

In his exposition of leadership, Andy Stanley begins with what he calls the two "best kept secrets" of leadership. The first is: "The less you do, the more you accomplish." The second follows: "The less you do, the more you enable others to accomplish." He states the obvious, "Every leader has authority over arenas in which he has little or no competence."[32] Hence, the leader should identify and encourage others to do the work with him.

LESSON OF THE EMPTY PARKING LOT

Thirdly, succession works with a leader who accepts his place. It must be hard for Moses to be told that he would not enter the Promised Land. Instead, he would join those of his generation, guilty of unbelief and disobedience, in the long funeral procession, dying one by one in the wilderness.

God had tempered the spirit of Moses, through challenges to his leadership by Miriam and by Korah.[33] Moses must have been torn between sharing the work with leaders who acknowledged his authority, and keeping the work from those who sought to undermine his authority. Yet, through it all, Moses emerged as "very meek, more than all people who were on the face of the earth."[34] Such meekness would have helped him accept that his time was up, and his role was over. So after a lifetime of service, he stepped down, having learned one of the most valuable lessons of life: no one is indispensable in God's service.

God never expects us to take on more than we can handle. God never intends us to build our work around ourselves. God forbid that we should view our position or role as indispensable. Eugene Peterson pastored Christ Our King Presbyterian Church, a congregation of 300, in Bel Air, Maryland, for 23 years before he took a year's sabbatical. He and the congregation suffered a measure of anxiety about how the church would get along without their pastor. When he returned after a year's absence, he related an incident:

> "About twenty-five of us were going on an overnight leadership retreat. We had agreed to meet in the church parking lot at 5:45 to car-pool together. I made a hospital visit that took longer than planned and arrived five minutes late—to an empty parking lot. They had left me. Before the sabbatical, that would never have happened; now that kind of thing happens all the time. They can take care of themselves and know that I can take care of myself."[35]

During his sabbatical, the church had learned to do things without their pastor—he was no longer indispensable. Instead of getting upset, he gave thanks to God. The church was no longer about him; it no longer revolved around him. To make succession happen, we must first unlearn our obsession to be busy and our compulsion to do everything. We serve our people best when we show them how to take care of themselves.

MOSES
For Reflection and Discussion

1. How is a busy leader considered by people? How can busyness be a good thing as well as a bad thing?

2. Why did Moses feel that he had to meet the people, and help them with their problems? How did his father-in-law, Jethro, view the situation?

3. What did Moses miss when he had three men helping him in the battle against the Amalekites? Did he eventually learn his lesson about doing everything himself?

4. Do you agree with the statement, "The less you do, the more you accomplish"? How is it true or untrue?

5. Reflect on Eugene Peterson's experience of the empty parking lot. How would you have felt if you were him?

Chapter Two

Joshua
Can Faith Last To The Third Generation?

"Wealth does not last three generations." So the Chinese say. With their thousands of years of recorded history, who can challenge their wisdom? Simply put, wealth will not stay in a family till the third generation. Only those who work hard to acquire riches appreciate its value. Those who inherit it often waste it. Does that apply also to faith? Are first-generation believers more likely to cherish their faith and pass it on, and are subsequent generations more likely to squander it?

History tells many stories of faith lost over time, by families and churches, and by whole communities. In a coal mining district of Loughor near Swansea in Wales, 26-year-old Evans Roberts began his ministry and sparked a revival. In the spring of 1904, he had been repeatedly awakened at 1.00 am, and spent time in prayer till 5.00 am. In November that year, Moriah Chapel was filled to capacity for a prayer meeting that lasted till 3.00 am. Through young Roberts, what is now known as the Welsh Revival of 1904-05 swept through the area. The revival transformed the whole community with churches packed and pubs emptied, sale of Bibles soaring and crime rate plunging. A judge sighed that he had few cases to try, and a tavern owner could sell only 9 cents of liquor on a Saturday night.

Coal miners crowded churches to pray till the early hours of the morning, then washed, ate breakfast, and returned to work, their employers amazed at the improved quality of work and attitude. Even the horses at the mines, it was said, were puzzled when their masters stopped spewing curses. By the following year, the powerful spiritual awakening had seen 100,000 people converted to Christ. The dramatic events captured headlines in newspapers, and the revival fire spread as far as Leeds in England and Edinburgh in Scotland.[36]

At the turn of the millennium, when the centenary of the revival was commemorated, the churches that witnessed the Welsh Revival looked back to it as a cherished piece of history. But their congregations today are a shadow of what they were then. The Sunday services attract a handful of elderly folks who still remember stories told by their parents and grandparents. What happened to the faith that brought thousands to their knees in prayer, and forged tens of thousands into a community that impacted the nation? That faith did not last beyond a couple of generations.[37] The same may be said of Joshua and the faith he inherited from Moses.

FEARS FOR THE NEXT GENERATION

Joshua assumed leadership of Israel at an elaborate handing-over ceremony. His predecessor Moses, as a last public act, entrusted the Book of the Law to the Levites, and recited a Song to be deposited with the people.[38] The charge to Joshua was affirming: "Be strong and courageous, for you shall go with this people into the land that the LORD has sworn to their fathers to give them…. It is the LORD who goes before you…."[39] But the words to the people sounded ominous:

> "For when I have brought them into the land flowing with milk and honey, which I swore to give to their fathers, and they have eaten and are full and grown fat, they will turn to other gods and serve them, and despise me and break my covenant.

> "For I know how rebellious and stubborn you are. Behold, even today while I am yet alive with you, you have been

rebellious against the LORD. How much more after my death!"[40]

Even before he took his leave, Moses feared for the next generation. How would his successor fare with the unbelief and rebellion which so marked the past generation? Would a change of environment from the wilderness to the Promised Land alleviate or aggravate the situation? Such concerns must weigh heavily on Moses' heart as he concluded with these words:

> "Take to heart all the words by which I am warning you today, that you may command them to your children, that they may be careful to do all the words of this law. For it is no empty word for you, but your very life, and by this word you shall live long in the land that you are going over the Jordan to possess."[41]

If Moses' concern extended only to the children of the emerging generation, then Joshua heard it well, and heeded it. As history testifies, Joshua kept his faith, and so did the elders who served with him. Fast forward one generation, and we witness another scene, similar to the first. Joshua—"old and well advanced in years"—summoned the leaders of Israel together, and charged them.[42] Then He gathered the leaders again, this time with the people and challenged them all to remain faithful to God as God had been faithful to them.[43]

When we consider the scene with Moses and the ones with Joshua, we see a glaring difference. Moses handed his leadership to Joshua, but Joshua handed his leadership to no one, at least to no one in particular. We see many parallels between the lives of two leaders. Moses parted the waters of the Red Sea, Joshua the waters of River Jordan. Both met with God who told them to remove their sandals. Both wrote the Law on stone.[44] Both closed their lives with stirring testimonies and rousing challenges. Why then did Joshua leave out the appointment of a successor?

One answer could be that God did not command him to do so.
To Moses, God named his successor. To Joshua, nothing was said. But
neither did God tell Joshua to hand his leadership to a coalition of
elders. Why did Joshua do what he did? A clue may be found in his
final act: "So Joshua sent the people away, every man to his
inheritance."[45] Immediately following that, the historian records
Joshua's death and burial "in his own inheritance at Timnath-serah."[46]

Thus the historian assures us that Joshua had accomplished his
mission—which was two-fold: to take the land from its inhabitants
and to settle his people in the land. As a military commander he
achieved the first, and as an organisational leader he fulfilled the
second. About midpoint in the Book of Joshua, we are told:

> "Now Joshua was old and advanced in years, and the LORD
> said to him, 'You are old and advanced in years, and there
> remains yet very much land to possess…. Only allot the
> land to Israel for an inheritance, as I have commanded
> you. Now therefore divide this land for an inheritance to
> the nine tribes and half the tribe of Manasseh.'"[47]

DISMISSAL TO EACH HIS OWN

God made it clear to Joshua that his fighting days were over,
despite the land yet to be conquered. The allotment of land to the
tribes would be his next and final duty. With that done, Joshua relieved
himself of his position and dismissed "every man to his inheritance."
The "every man" included himself as he lay to rest in his own
inheritance. Two developments seem to have arisen from this outcome.
Firstly, we see a shift towards a decentralised society. No longer was
one supreme leader needed to lead the whole nation; every tribe had
its land and its leaders: "its elders and heads, its judges and officers."[48]
Could this be the reason why Joshua saw no need to appoint a successor?

Secondly, we see a shift towards a settled life. As with Moses,
Joshua had expressed concern for the future of his people. His closing

words to them contained dire warnings against serving other gods.[49] Did he fear that transitioning from a battle-ready people to a land-sitting people would take the fighting spirit out of them, and leave them weakened against foreign influence? Whatever was in the mind of Joshua when he relinquished his command, we know that the faith he inherited from the generation of Moses made it only to the second but not the third generation. The end of Joshua's era and the beginning of the next tell the sad truth:

> "Israel served the LORD all the days of Joshua, and all the days of the elders who outlived Joshua and had known all the work that the LORD did for Israel."

> "And all that generation also were gathered to their fathers. And there arose another generation after them who did not know the LORD or the work that he had done for Israel. And the people of Israel did what was evil in the sight of the LORD and served the Baals."[50]

So the rule of the elders passed on to the rule of the judges, a period made notorious by the damning verdict: "In those days there was no king in Israel. Everyone did what was right in his own eyes."[51] When we remember how everyone went his way to his own inheritance, we wonder if that could have sown the seed for everyone to go his own way. Whoever delivered the foregoing verdict on the period of the judges dropped a loud hint that the situation arose because of the lack of a single, strong, kingly leader. He might have well laid the responsibility for this at the feet of Joshua.

In his study of leadership succession in the Bible, Perry L. Stepp laments,

> "The story of Israel after Joshua is a story of the failure of leadership. Joshua did not provide for the leadership of future generations, nor did the judges. The same cycle of

sin and punishment plays out over and over. Israel falls
away from the commitment to Yahweh after the death of
Joshua and his generation…."[52]

Stepp points to the judges after Joshua: Ehud, Jair, and Abdon,
and observes,

"In none of these cases, nor in any other case, are we told
of any provision for succession of leadership after the death
of these or other leaders. No one followed the example of
Moses, and—from the perspective of Judges—Israel
suffered for the lack of leadership as a result."[53]

Moses took certain precautions: he placed the Law in the hands
of the Levites and a song in the hearts of the people. These could have
kept alive the memory of God's saving acts in Joshua's generation. To
be fair, Joshua did at Shechem what Moses did at the plains of Moab:
spelling out the demands of the Law, and setting it up as a witness
against the people.[54] But without a successor, the similarity ends.

The challenges faced by Moses and by Joshua are different, and
so are their leadership styles. We should not be quick to judge Moses
as right and Joshua as wrong when it comes to leadership succession.
We will never know if the appointment of a successor would have
helped take the faith of Israel to the third generation and beyond. At
the tail-end of the period of judges, the prophet-priest-judge Samuel
would emerge as the principal leader and king-maker. Thereafter, Israel
would be ruled by kings—for better or for worse.

NO LINGERING IN THE SHADOWS

As a case-study in leadership succession, Joshua presents us with
a number of lessons. Firstly, at a time of transition, a leader needs to
establish his credibility. By all accounts, the succession of Joshua from
Moses worked. Joshua had the endorsement of his predecessor. Within

a short time, he proved himself a worthy successor when he led the people across the River Jordan. He earned the confidence of his followers. Most important of all, Moses had stepped aside, leaving the people with no choice but to follow Joshua.

Had Moses remained, even in the shadows, the succession would not have worked. Many succession plans have fallen apart because the predecessor lingered around. The latter may not wish to interfere, but the people hanker for his return at the slightest unhappiness with the new leader. To make succession work, the predecessor must remove himself, physically and emotionally, from the scene. At every opportunity, he must refer the people to his successor, and at no time, give the impression he is still in charge.

When John R. W. Stott, after a long and distinguished ministry as rector of All Souls Church in London, decided to step down, his chosen successor, Michael Baughen, wondered if it would work. The leaders of the church approached the Bishop of London, Robert Stopford, for advice.

> "[The Bishop] ...agreed with Michael that the plan wouldn't work if John retained leadership of the church, with the people appealing to him to overrule Michael if they disagreed with his leadership. So Stopford worked out a scheme to hand over all leadership of the church to Michael, with John just retaining the power to sign any legal papers as Rector."[55]

John also stopped attending staff meetings which were now led by Michael. Years later, Michael would attribute the smooth transition to John: "I am convinced that the unusual arrangement would not have worked without John's humility, his utter refusal to listen to any complaints and his total support of me."[56] Unfortunately, not every leader is blessed with such humility and resolve to make succession work for his successor. In any transition in leadership, the incoming leader must establish his credibility and win the people's confidence. His predecessor can make or break that process.

Secondly, in times of crisis, people need strong leadership vested in one person. The deliverance from Egypt needed a Moses, and the campaign in Canaan a Joshua. After Joshua, crisis gave way to routine as the people settled in the land. In such a situation, leadership tends to devolve from a person to a panel. So Joshua left no successor except the elders. Such a change meant less central control and more local autonomy. In the generation after Joshua, it also meant anarchy.

In the life-span of an organisation, the pioneering stage usually features a sole and strong leader. As the organisation grows and establishes itself, the leader divests his authority to a board. As long as the board provides clear leadership, the organisation moves forward. If, however, factions arise and split the leadership, the organisation stops growing. Or else, a maintenance mode sets in, and everybody's business becomes nobody's business; growth reaches a plateau. At this stage, a strong leader must arise to break the impasse.[57]

Wise succession planning discerns when autocratic leadership is needed, and when democratic leadership serves better. I once sat in a search committee for a church whose pastor had resigned. I asked the elders if they were looking for a prophet or a priest. A prophet would be someone who takes charge, speaks authoritatively, and leads decisively. A priest would be someone who comes down to the level of the people, shepherds them and leads them gently along. The elders wisely discerned the needs of the church at that time, and opted for the latter. We found a priestly pastor who went on to lead the church for many years.

FLAT WORLD AND JET STREAM

In a different situation, a prophetic leader may be needed, such as when a church or organisation is embroiled in protracted controversies.

Someone with clarity of vision and a voice of authority may be the person of the hour. Joshua stepped in as such a leader. With a land to conquer and a people to settle, the situation demanded no less. After him, the leadership structure flattened out. The elders took over, each for his own tribe and land. Our world today seems to favour such flat, spread-out, ground-up leadership. But as we have seen, such a flat world can lead to each person doing what is right in his or her own eyes.

The advent of the Internet has precipitated the process of flattening the world. Information once safeguarded by a few is now freely and instantly available to the masses. *Encyclopedia Britannica,* once written by experts, has given way to *Wikipedia,* written by ordinary contributors. Anyone can broadcast himself or herself on *Youtube.* Everyone has a voice and may speak with equal authority. Hierarchy has collapsed to a flat line.

> "The genesis of the flat-world platform not only enabled more people to author more content, and to collaborate on that content. It also enabled them to upload files and globalize that content—individually or as part of self-forming communities—without going through any of the traditional hierarchical organizations or institutions."[58]

Another analogy has been used to describe the different leadership styles in the succession process: the "runway" leaders who give way to the "jet stream" leaders. Patrick Lambe illustrates this with the picture of a plane taking off. The aircraft burns the bulk of its fuel during takeoff from the runway. When it reaches cruising speed, fuel efficiency kicks in—the air is thinner and friction is lower. If the tail-wind works in the plane's favour, fuel consumption is reduced further. Leaders taking the plane off the runway consume more fuel and expend more effort, while leaders in the jet stream go farther on less fuel. The temptation for leaders who inherit their position in mid-flight is to ride on the success of their predecessors and to become complacent.[59] This could have happened to the generation after Joshua—which leads us to the final lesson we can draw from our case-study.

Finally, when a crisis is past, people need to stay alert. When our church bought a piece of land and embarked on a building project, our people rallied around it with immense excitement. Like the children of Israel, we had wandered from place to place, meeting in borrowed facilities. After almost two decades, we were going into a place and a building of our own! Yet, as I reflected on the move, I was filled with trepidation. I remembered how, at two points of Israel's history, the people fell away from God: when they entered a land of their own, and when they built the temple. Within a generation after Joshua, Israel had backslidden—it happened again within a generation after Solomon.

While succession worked for Joshua, and he finished well, it did not augur well for those after him. People living in post-crisis time let down their guard and succumb to complacency. Having settled in the Promised Land, the people forgot God, ignored his warnings, defied his commands, adopted pagan practices and served other gods. Appropriately, at the ground-claiming ceremony of our building project, elder statesman Bobby Sng issued a warning, "When you settle into a place of your own, be careful that your forward look does not become an inward look."[60]

The inward look leads easily to a narcissistic complex with everyone "doing what is right in his own eyes." The challenge that rallies everyone together has passed. Perhaps that was what happened to the Welsh Revival of 1904-05. It came and went. On the website for tourists visiting Wales, the National Library Exhibition is recommended with the following note:

> "The Revival also led to a small industry in booklets, articles, postcards and pamphlets chronicling the latest events, many of which are in the collection of the National

Library, which is holding an exhibition to commemorate this centenary. The Library collection also contains Evan Roberts' original Bible, which he took daily to the Broad Oak coalmine, Loughor."

So the faith that began in the hearts of coal-miners failed to make it to a subsequent generation, and instead found its way into a museum viewed by curious tourists. Succession, left to chance and the forces of nature, will not work. If we do not cherish our faith enough to pass it on, we stand to lose it all by the third generation.

JOSHUA
For Reflection and Discussion

1.   What is the main point of the Chinese saying, "Wealth does not last three generations"? How does it apply to what happened after the Welsh Revival of 1904-05?

2.   Unlike Moses, Joshua did not appoint a successor when he stepped down as the leader of Israel. Instead, he handed his leadership to the elders of the different tribes. Why did he do that, and how did it affect the future generation of Israel?

3.   At the point when Joshua needed his predecessor most, Moses was taken away. How did the absence of Moses help or hinder the succession process from one leader to the other?

4.   It is said of the generation after the elders that "Everyone did what was right in his own eyes." Is that a description of the world today? Discuss how the "flattening" of the world with the advent of the Internet has affected us.

5.   What happens when a crisis is past? What can we do to avoid falling into complacency and losing our heritage?

Chapter Three

The Levites
Should We Retire at Fifty?

The founding pastor of our denomination had said it more than once, "I do not believe in retirement in God's service." In the Bible College which he founded and where I studied, I had it drummed into me. So today I too say, "I do not believe in retirement in God's service." But I do believe in succession—and succession requires a role change tied to age.

In 1989, after editing *Far Eastern Economic Review* for almost three decades, Derek Davies pointed to one curse that remained in the region: that of old men who cling to power and refuse to retire.[61] Twenty years on, in 2010, George B.N. Ayittey of Ghana writing for *Foreign Policy Magazine*, echoes that same indictment. He names 23 of "the worst of the worst" dictators, among them, Kim Jong Il of North Korea, Mugabe of Zimbabwe, Than Shwe of Burma, Al-Bashir of Sudan, Mubarak of Egypt and Al-Qaddafi of Libya—these six have held power for a total of 155 years.

> "Although all dictators are bad in their own way, there's one insidious aspect of despotism that is most infuriating and galling to me: the disturbing frequency with which many despots... began their careers as erstwhile *freedom fighters* who were supposed to have liberated their people.... So familiar are Africans with this phenomenon that we

have [a] saying: 'We struggle very hard to remove one cockroach from power, and the next rat comes to do the same thing.'"[62]

They started well, but overstayed their tenure. Such leaders have several things in common: they wield considerable power, they rule into their old age, and they refuse to step down from their position once they got into it. As a result, the good they achieved in the earlier years of their office became undone. Had they retired at the right time with the right successor, their countries would have suffered less turmoil and hardship, and realised more stability and prosperity. These leaders did not believe in retirement, neither did they believe in succession.

The Bible says little or nothing about retirement. Many of God's faithful servants served into their ripe old age. Moses stepped down from office only when the Lord called him home. Samuel served as prophet and priest till, in his own words, he became "old and gray."[63] David ruled as king till he died. Daniel served through the reign of four kings spanning seven decades. Paul wrote letters from prison to his congregations as he awaited execution.

Though the word "retirement" is never used of such men, nor the examples of retirement ever cited, one biblical passage lays down the principle of a role change linked to age. The ESV titles the paragraph, *Retirement of the Levites*.[64]

"And the LORD spoke to Moses, saying, 'This applies to the Levites: from twenty-five years old and upward they shall come to do duty in the service of the tent of meeting. And from the age of fifty years they shall withdraw from the duty of the service and serve no more. They minister to their brothers in the tent of meeting by keeping guard, but they shall do no service. Thus shall you do to the Levites in assigning their duties.'"[65]

The LORD spells out the lower and upper limits of actively serving Levites. As regards the lower limit, a Levite must be at least 25 years of age to serve in the tent of meeting. The age rises to 30 in some references,[66] and drops to 20 in others.[67] This disparity has spawned various explanations. The period between 20 or 25 to 30 could have been an apprenticeship. The age limit could have been lowered to enlist more Levites to meet the growing demands of a settled population.[68]

We cannot know for sure, but the Chronicler gives us a hint when he noted the transition from a movable tabernacle in the wilderness to a permanent one in Jerusalem.

"These were the sons of Levi by their fathers' houses, the heads of fathers' houses as they were listed according to the number of the names of the individuals from twenty years old and upward who were to do the work for the service of the house of the LORD. For David said, 'The LORD, the God of Israel, has given rest to his people, and he dwells in Jerusalem forever. And so the Levites no longer need to carry the tabernacle or any of the things for its service.' For by the last words of David the sons of Levi were numbered from twenty years old and upward."[69]

When the tabernacle had to be set up, taken down and transported, older Levites were needed. One would have thought that for such strenuous work, younger Levites would have been better employed. Perhaps, the reference here is not only to the physical work but also the spiritual nature of the work. Uzzah was struck dead when he handled the transportation of the ark in a manner unacceptable to God.[70] Surely, more mature Levites would be better placed to handle such sacred artefacts belonging to the place of worship.

UPPER LIMIT FOR LOWER CLASS?

While the lower limit varies, the upper limit remains constant at fifty.[71] To understand such a limit, we turn to the work of the Levites which is described as "to do the work for the service of the house of the LORD," "to assist the sons of Aaron for the service of the house of the LORD," and "to keep charge of the tent of meeting and the sanctuary, and to attend the sons of Aaron, their brothers, for the service of the house of the LORD."[72] The duties come in general terms, and fall into the category of supporting services.

With such a job description, commentators have assessed their work as "drudgery," "servile and menial," and in other similar terms.[73] Perhaps, such sentiments arise when we think of the work of a church janitor or warden. He keeps the premises clean and secure, unlocks and locks rooms, arranges chairs for meetings, switches on and off lights, ensures supplies are in stock, knows where everything is kept, attends to enquiries and requests, and so on. Every pastor knows the important role such a warden plays. Without him, the pastor will be overwhelmed with a myriad of logistical details, not to mention the onslaught of complaints by church members.

Though the role of the Levites appears menial, they provide vital support for the priests.[74] The Levites take care of "the courts and the chambers, the cleansing of all that is holy" and ensure supplies and quality control as they "assist with the showbread, the flour for the grain offering, the wafers of unleavened bread, the baked offering, the offering mixed with oil, and all measures of quantity or size."[75] Moreover, they assume the privileged trust and function of praising God in the sanctuary, "to stand every morning, thanking and praising the LORD, and likewise at evening...."[76]

As we will see in Asaph, one of the Levites, such an honoured tradition would be passed down through the generations. At each high point of the nation's long history, their service would be enlisted and their presence highlighted. We meet them at the dedication as well as the restoration of the temple, the dedication of the new city wall, and the foundation-laying for the new temple.[77] The role given to the Levites is far from ordinary and mundane. Their calling is one marked by dignity and distinction.

However important their role may be, the Levites assist the priests; they do not do the work of the priests. The differentiation between the two may be seen in the way they are inducted into the ministry and the way they serve. Unlike the priests, the Levites receive no special anointing with blood at their initiation. Unlike the priests, they wear no special vestments to set them apart from the people. [78] One commentator describes them as a "bridge" between the priests and the people.[79]

Indeed, as the priests represent the people to God, so the Levites represent the people to the priests. Not all the people can serve the priests, so the Levites are chosen to take their places.

"Thus you shall separate the Levites from among the people of Israel, and the Levites shall be mine... For all the firstborn among the people of Israel are mine, both of man and of beast. On the day that I struck down all the firstborn in the land of Egypt I consecrated them for myself, and I have taken the Levites instead of all the firstborn among the people of Israel. And I have given the Levites as a gift to Aaron and his sons from among the people of Israel, to do the service for the people of Israel at the tent of meeting...."[80]

God has taken the Levites from the people as his own, so that he can give them "as a gift" to Aaron and the priests. God also underlines the special status of the Levites by exempting them from any inheritance of the land given to all the other tribes of Israel.[81] So as not to have this viewed as a deprivation, God himself pledges personally to provide for them, "You shall have no inheritance in their land, neither shall you have any portion among them. I am your portion and your inheritance among the people of Israel."[82]

For practical purposes, the tribe of Levi could not all live in one place. Since they, the Levites, had been chosen by God to serve the whole community of Israel, they had to be scattered among all the other tribes. So instead of land, they were allocated cities, 48 in all, located among the tribes.[83] These included the six cities of refuge to which a person who had killed someone accidentally might flee and seek sanctuary till such time he was given a fair trial. Again, in such matters of life and death, the role of the Levites comes into prominent focus.

AIRLINE PILOT, SURGEON AND EVENT-PLANNER

The Levites are subordinate to the priests in role, but not inferior to them in importance. As such, we wonder why a retirement age is set for the Levites, and not for the priests. How do we extrapolate from such a requirement, spelled out so clearly as a divine directive? Do we argue from the lesser to the greater? If so, then priests should have a retirement age too. If an assistant to an airline pilot should work no more than so many hours at a stretch, the pilot would be kept to a stricter limit. Likewise, would be a surgeon in an operating theatre if the assisting nurse has to be relieved after working a specified number of hours. By this argument the priest would be retired too, and by a more stringent measure.

However, we can take other lines of argument. If we consider the work of the priests as essentially "spiritual" and the work of the Levites as "administrative" we may argue that greater continuity is required of the priesthood than of the supporting cast. In a local church, the change of the pastor would send more waves than the loss of an administrative staff. In the same way, it may be easier to fill in a backstage crew than a lead singer. One, being more upfront and visible, may need to stay around longer than the other.

The argument could also be turned around. The work of the Levites may be more demanding. The priests merely show up and carry out their duties. The Levites set up the place, prepare all that is needed, then clear up when it is all over. People in the event-planning industry know what it takes to set up an event, run it, and then take it down afterwards. The work involves long and unearthly hours, seemingly impossible deadlines, conflicting demands from different parties, and many other variables. No wonder, those in the industry are often young with a ready stock of physical energy and stamina. If so, then a retirement age for the Levites makes sense. Their work being more strenuous requires a fresh supply of the younger Levites.

What are some principles we can draw from the mandatory retirement age for the Levites? Firstly, it speaks of the humane laws God has set in place for those serving him. These laws reflect the compassion and consideration that God shows towards working people. Human employers are likely to work their employees to death, whereas God draws a line to say, Enough. For the Levites, the age of 50 is the finishing line of their service. Thereafter, they may in good conscience step aside for others to take over, "to be loaded with the honours of their office, as hitherto they had been with the burdens of it."[84]

Secondly, it tells us that God wants us to serve him in the prime of our lives.[85] When identifying leaders for training at Haggai Institute, we target those in their early forties as leaders with the greatest potential to impact others. They have enough of years behind them for experience, and enough of years ahead for service. The Levites, in offering God the years between 30 and 50, gave of their best years. This is in contrast to those who choose ministry as a second career later in life or after they retire from success in the corporate world.

Thirdly, the role change enforced on the Levites ensures a succession of younger Levites in service. The ones beyond the age of 50 do not abdicate their responsibility. They merely change their role, from doing the work to assisting those who now do the work. This shift provides the critical impetus to succession. Strictly speaking, the older Levites did not retire from service. They became mentors to the younger Levites. They continued to serve but in a different capacity: "they shall withdraw from the duty of the service and serve no more. They minister to their brothers in the tent of meeting by keeping guard, but they shall do no service."[86]

TRANSITION TO GOALKEEPERS AND GATEKEEPERS

As the Levites assist the priests and do not presume to do their work, so the older Levites assist the younger Levites and refrain from doing the work for them. This completes the succession process which begins with the older doing it while the younger watches, and ends with the younger doing it while the older looks on. The language used here appears military: the Levites are said to have ceased from warfare, but continue to stand guard.[87] A modern equivalent could be that of a striker in the soccer line-up transitioning to a goalkeeper or a coach. In organisational life, a founder-president may move into an advisory position and assume the role of a gatekeeper of the organisation's vision and mission. Whichever way we perceive it, succession rules. Vitality and maturity, youthful energy and tested wisdom—all work together to make succession succeed.

The issue of retirement in the service of God will continue to be debated. On the one hand, there are those who refuse to let go. On the other hand, there are those who let go too soon. Both do harm to the work of God. We do well to think of service without attaching it to a position. A position can be occupied and vacated, but service goes on. To step down from a position does not necessarily mean to step out of service.

A.W. Tozer began serving at Southside Alliance Church in Chicago at the age of 31 years. Three decades later, at the age of 62, he tendered his resignation. He gave two reasons: firstly, he felt called to "certain spiritual labours" which the pastoral ministry did not allow him time to pursue; secondly, the proposed relocation of the church demanded "a different kind of minister." But he insisted he was not retiring from God's service:

> "I'll preach as long as I can hold a Bible. [The priests of Israel] began their ministry when they were 30 and finished it when they were 50. Thus they had only 20 years of active ministry. But prophets never retired, so I'm not retiring, except to put on new tires to go a little faster and farther."[88]

Tozer moved on to Avenue Road Church in Toronto where, with no other duties, he preached twice each Sunday to a packed sanctuary, and completed writing his landmark book, *The Knowledge of the Holy*. He also had the joy of preaching the dedication sermon at the new building of his former church. Tozer did not believe in retirement, but he did believe in a change of role tied to his age. He believed in succession, and practised it to the blessing of all.

THE LEVITES
For Reflection and Discussion

1.   How do you respond to someone who says, "I do not believe in retirement—I intend to serve until I die"?

2.   The mandatory retirement age of fifty was required of the Levites. What is the principle behind this divine directive? Does it apply to those who are not Levites?

3.   Describe the work of the Levites. How is it different from the work of the priests? Why do you think Levites were mandated to start working at thirty and stop working at fifty?

4.   Levites do not stop working completely at fifty. They were required to continue to assist the younger Levites in their duties. What do you think are the benefits of such an arrangement?

5.   Discuss how our role can change as we grow older. How would this work out in your family, organisation, business, or church?

Chapter Four

Asaph
Can A Legacy Endure 400 Years?

Victor Hugo told the story in 1862. More than a hundred years later, in 1980, Alain Boublil and Claude-Michel Schönberg re-told it in music and set it on stage. Their French original made its English debut in London in 1985. *Les Misérables* has since run for 25 years, watched by millions in cities, languages and cultures as diverse as Buenos Aires to Tel Aviv, Helsinki to Tokyo.

Another epic, *The Ramayana,* originating in the 11ᵗʰ century in India, re-emerged on the Hindu island of Bali around 1930 as a dance. Known as the *kecak* dance, it is performed by a hundred men, chanting and gesticulating to pulsating music, portraying the cosmic battle between Prince Rama and the evil king Ravana. It has fascinated audiences from all over the world for eight decades.

What is it about music and drama that gives the combination such an enduring character? A musical, a dance or a play could go on and on, appreciated and honoured, remembered and cherished. We tell and re-tell a story, we hear and hear it again. We watch it, and invite others to watch it. Thus stories like *Les Misérables and The Ramayana* are passed on. What better way to pass tradition from one community to another, one generation to another!

In the generations that span the pages of the Old Testament, one name stands out as someone who successfully passed on his legacy to those after him. His name is easily missed because it usually appears as one of many names in a list. Yet, it occurs often enough, over a sufficiently long period, for us to take notice. The name is Asaph.

We first encounter him as the son of Berechiah, who traced his family line back to Gershon, one of the sons of Levi.[89] That makes him a Levite. His name could mean "he who gathers" or "he who is gathered (by the Lord)" though we are uncertain if the root is even Hebrew. We do know he stood out in music. When King David brought the ark of God to Jerusalem, he instructed the leaders of the Levites to assign singers and musicians to celebrate the occasion. Asaph, together with Heman and Ethan, were appointed as the leading musicians, sounding the bronze cymbals.[90]

FATHERS AND SONS BONDING

Asaph must have caught the attention of the king, for when the ark was settled in the city, he was promoted to become David's chief musician. In the record of his appointment, Asaph's name is mentioned three times, each time preceding other names. By now, he is clearly the leader of the worship music ministry at the tent of meeting.

> "Then he [David] appointed some of the Levites as ministers before the ark of the LORD, to invoke, to thank, and to praise the LORD, the God of Israel. *Asaph* was the chief, and second to him were Zechariah, Jeiel, Shemiramoth, Jehiel, Mattithiah, Eliab, Benaiah, Obed-edom, and Jeiel, who were to play harps and lyres; *Asaph* was to sound the cymbals, and Benaiah and Jahaziel the priests were to blow trumpets regularly before the ark of the covenant of God. Then on that day David first appointed that thanksgiving be sung to the LORD by *Asaph* and his brothers."[91]

Along with Asaph, two other leading musicians are mentioned: Heman and Ethan (also known as Jeduthun). Interestingly, these two were assigned to another place, Gibeon, an important worship place which in time would be overshadowed by Jerusalem.[92] In time, King David, in consultation with his military leaders, organised the singers and musicians into ranks and orders, with each name meticulously recorded.[93] Of note in the long lists of names is the mention of "the sons of Asaph" and the sons of others, together with this telling piece of information:

> "All these men were under the supervision of their fathers for the music of the temple of the LORD, with cymbals, lyres and harps, for the ministry at the house of God.... Along with their relatives—all of them trained and skilled in music for the LORD—they numbered 288. Young and old alike, teacher as well as student, cast lots for their duties."[94]

Asaph had taken a step back, and his sons had begun to serve. As a Levite, he would have been aware of the mandatory retirement age laid down as a divine directive.[95] Had Asaph, having reached 50 years of age, withdrawn from active service and taken on the role of a mentor and trainer? It appears to be so, as we read of fathers and sons, "young and old alike, teacher as well as student" working together— one learning and the other teaching. If so, this would explain how the legacy of Asaph was passed on to his sons, and his grandsons. As Don DeVries rightly observes in The Legacy of Asaph – Fathers Training Sons,

> "For nearly 500 years, Asaph and his sons and grandsons and great-grandsons and great-great grandsons and on down the line knew and followed the Lord, serving Him faithfully in worship and praise and prophecy."[96]

Here is how we know the living legacy of Asaph as we trace it down the generations, starting from his own. When Solomon succeeded his father David as king, he fulfilled his predecessor's dream of building a temple for the Lord. At the grand dedication of the temple, the sons of Asaph, together with those of two other families, took centre stage

> "...and all the Levitical singers, Asaph, Heman, and Jeduthun, their sons and kinsmen, arrayed in fine linen, with cymbals, harps, and lyres, stood east of the altar with 120 priests who were trumpeters; and it was the duty of the trumpeters and singers to make themselves heard in unison in praise and thanksgiving to the LORD), and when the song was raised, with trumpets and cymbals and other musical instruments, in praise to the LORD, 'For he is good, for his steadfast love endures forever,' the house, the house of the LORD was filled with a cloud... for the glory of the LORD filled the house of God."[97]

WORD OF PROPEHCY IN SONG

Asaph's ministry proved as enduring as God's love. A hundred years later, the succession of kings brings us to the reign of King Jehoshaphat. A crisis gripped the kingdom as a coalition of armies of the Moabites and Ammonites threatened war against the king and his people. The Chronicler paints for us a poignant scene of "the men of Judah, with their wives and children and little ones"[98] standing with the king, waiting for a word from the Lord. In that hour of need, a prophetic word came from Jahaziel who is described as "a Levite of the sons of Asaph."[99]

We have learned earlier that the music ministry of Asaph and his sons encompass a prophetic ministry as well. At the time of King David, the sons of Asaph "prophesied with lyres, with harps, and with cymbals" and they, under the tutelage of Asaph, "prophesied under the direction of the king."[100] Clearly, the music they made was not simply music or merely a form. The music served as a vehicle for truths preached and prophesied.[101] The practice continued till the time of

King of Jehoshaphat when the word of God came through a descendant of Asaph. True to the tradition Asaph represented, the subsequent victory over the invading armies incorporated worship in song and music:

> " And when he [King Jehoshaphat] had taken counsel with the people, he appointed those who were to sing to the LORD and praise him in holy attire, as they went before the army, and say, 'Give thanks to the LORD, for his steadfast love endures forever.' And when they began to sing and praise, the LORD set an ambush against the men of Ammon, Moab, and Mount Seir, who had come against Judah, so that they were routed."[102]

Another 140 years passed, and we come to the reign of King Hezekiah. The mighty acts of God forgotten, the people languished in spiritual darkness. As Hezekiah began his rule, he opened the doors of the temple to expose the years of neglect. He brought together the priests and the Levites and called on them to restore worship to its rightful place in the temple and in the nation. As we have come to expect, the sons or descendants of Asaph, were among those enlisted (italics added).

> "Then the Levites arose, Mahath the son of Amasai, and Joel the son of Azariah, of the sons of the Kohathites; and of the sons of Merari, Kish the son of Abdi, and Azariah the son of Jehallelel; and of the Gershonites, Joah the son of Zimmah, and Eden the son of Joah; and of the sons of Elizaphan, Shimri and Jeuel; and of *the sons of Asaph,* Zechariah and Mattaniah; and of the sons of Heman, Jehuel and Shimei; and of the sons of Jeduthun, Shemaiah and Uzziel. They gathered their brothers and consecrated themselves and went in as the king had commanded, by the words of the LORD, to cleanse the house of the LORD."[103]

More than two and a half centuries had passed since Asaph was appointed chief musician by King David. His legacy continues. Another 80 years bring us to the reign of King Josiah. The two kings between him and his great-grandfather Hezekiah had brought the kingdom to ruins. Manasseh had installed altars to foreign deities in the temple, and made idolatry the state religion.[104] His son Amon perpetuated the downward spiral into apostasy. This must leave us wondering what had happened to the sons of Asaph.

The answer comes as Josiah destroyed the idols, restored worship to the temple and re-instituted the celebration of the Passover. The occasion saw the offering of 32,600 Passover lambs and young goats, and 3,300 bulls for sacrifice. A commemoration of such scale would not be complete without music, and so we find the familiar faces reappearing: "The singers, the sons of Asaph, were in their place according to the command of David, and Asaph, and Heman, and Jeduthun the king's seer...."[105]

After close to a century of the people's unfaithfulness and forgetfulness, the sons of Asaph still remembered their standing position and their vital role in preserving the true worship of God. Another period of history would test the legacy of Asaph. The kingdom from the house of David finally fell apart and the people were taken in captivity by the Babylonians. Seventy years of geographical dislocation and foreign domination followed.

DON'T DROP THE BATON

After decades of humiliation, the people were allowed to return to their homeland. It had been over 400 years since Asaph took on his first assignment as the king's chief musician. Had his descendants survived the captivity, and if they did, do they still remember what their forefathers had done? Ezra and Nehemiah chronicled the return of the exiles, the rebuilding of the walls of Jerusalem and the restoration of worship to the city. Among the returnees were "the singers: the sons of Asaph" numbering 128.[106] Listed among those who lived in Jerusalem were (italics added):

> "And of the Levites: Shemaiah the son of Hasshub, son of Azrikam, son of Hashabiah, son of Bunni; and Shabbethai and Jozabad, of the chiefs of the Levites, who were over the outside work of the house of God; and Mattaniah the son of Mica, son of Zabdi, *son of Asaph,* who was the leader of the praise, who gave thanks, and Bakbukiah, the second among his brothers; and Abda the son of Shammua, son of Galal, son of Jeduthun. All the Levites in the holy city were 284."[107]

Though their numbers had been reduced from the thousands at Solomon's temple dedication to less than 200, they were present at the dedication of the rebuilt walls as well as at the foundation-laying for the second temple.[108] They were there, leading worship as they had done for centuries. Even the theme had not changed: "And they sang responsively, praising and giving thanks to the LORD, 'For he is good, for his steadfast love endures forever toward Israel.'"[109] The words are almost identical to what they sang at the dedication of the first temple built by Solomon. The legacy of Asaph had lived on and lasted for ten generations and more.

The baton that Asaph held was passed on to subsequent runners. In the Asian Games 2010 in Guangzhou, the Kazakhstan team never made it beyond their second runner in the women's relay race. The baton was dropped, and as the two runners slumped on the sideline, dejection on their faces, the commentator offered his sympathy, "It could happen to the best team." The slow motion footage showed the first runner trying to place the baton in the hand of the second, but missed, then the second runner feeling for the baton when it fell. Was it the fault of the one or the other, or of both?

In any succession, the handing-over can fail on the part of the predecessor or the successor, or both. Asaph and his line of descendants had mastered the art of placing the baton in the right place, and grasping it at the right moment. Could the mandatory retirement age for the Levites be a significant factor in such a seamless transition from one hand to another? All relay runners anticipate the point of hand-over, concentrating their minds and regulating their pace towards the one crucial act that could win or lose the race.

WRITING SONGS AND PLANTING TREES

The name of Asaph also appears as the author of 12 psalms in the Hebrew psalmody.[110] In the years of its compilation, the eponymous ancestor of the Levitical guild of singers could have written the psalms himself or lent his name to a repertoire or style in his honour. In his longest psalm, Asaph exploited poetic license to describe God as a man awaking from sleep or a drunk rousing from stupor. Perhaps, that was how Asaph saw the work of God portrayed in human terms: for a large part of the psalm, God seemed absent or dormant; then he "awoke as from sleep, as a man awakes from the stupor of wine."[111]

In the same way, the work of Asaph and his descendants never really ceased; it went into a "sleep mode" only to spring back to life each time it was needed. No wonder we see the sons of Asaph appearing again and again, from generation to generation, as expressed in the same psalm:

> "We will not hide them from their children, but tell to the coming generation the glorious deeds of the LORD, and his might, and the wonders that he has done. He established a testimony in Jacob and appointed a law in Israel, which he commanded our fathers to teach to their children, that the next generation might know them, the children yet unborn, and arise and tell them to their children..."[112]

How can we heed the call of Asaph to pass on a legacy of faith to the generations after us? We can begin by thinking in decades and generations instead of in months and years. Paul J. Meyer tells a story of someone who thought that way:

"I once heard of a church that was built around A.D. 1000. When it came time to replace the aging roof some two hundred years later, the original plans were brought and studied. There in the plans was a detailed note explaining where a forest had been planted at the time of the church's construction consisting of a specific type of tree that ought to be used for the roof's support beams.

"The trees were discovered exactly where the plans stated—*having been planted in neat rows 200 years earlier!* Only someone with a long-term mentality could have ever thought of planting a forest for a need that did not then exist!"[113]

How can we think and act in such dimensions? Asaph and his descendants have a few things to teach us. Firstly, the best place to preserve a legacy and pass it on is the family. Home is where all our stories begin. It is where these stories should be remembered, told and re-told till they become part of our collective memory. Asaph founded a legacy within his family, and it never left the family line. For this to happen, parents need to train their children when they are young. When the time comes, as it did for all Levites at the age of 50, the parents learn to step aside and let their children take over.

PACKAGING MUSIC AND MEMORY

Secondly, the best way to package and deliver a legacy is by music. When our church presented an original musical which we had written, we brought in the children. Though they sang in only one scene in the musical, they and their friends knew all the songs. I could see them mouthing the songs as they were performed on stage. At one point when a player lost his lines, a boy shouted it from the audience! They had memorised not only the song lyrics but the entire script. Such is the power of music to preserve what we desire to pass on.

In addition, the legacy of Asaph came packaged in order and routine. King David established the order of the singers and musicians in consultation with his military leaders.[114] Even a cursory reading of the lists of names impresses us with the way they were methodically organised and meticulously recorded. It certainly reminds us of the discipline and precision we associate with the military. This may explain how the sons of Asaph still remembered their places hundreds of years later.[115] Though musical people love innovation and shun regulation, it is eventually order and discipline that preserves what they create and pass on.

Finally, memory serves us best when high points of life are celebrated. Asaph and his descendants ministered at various times, but each occasion marked some significant landmark of the nation's history: the dedication of the temple, the threat of war, the purification of the temple, the restoration of a festival, the dedication of the city wall, and the foundation of a new temple. Asaph sings of "the glorious deeds of the LORD, and his might, and the wonders that he has done" so that "children yet unborn" may know and remember.[116] We do well to commemorate significant events of our community, our church, and our family.

We have seen how music can help preserve a legacy and pass it on. A musical did it for *Les Misérables* and a dance did it for *The Ramayana*. But few modern examples can match one that goes back to the small village of Oberammergau in Germany. Bubonic plague struck and took the lives of villagers from October 1632 to July 1633. The deaths stopped when the village vowed they would perform the *Passion of Christ* every ten years should they be spared. From 1634 onwards, for almost 400 years (with two rare exceptions), the whole village has come together to fulfill their promise.

Started in the 17th century, the legacy has continued into the 21st century. Today each performance involves 2000 players and lasts seven hours. In the course of five months, the 102 performances attract half a million visitors. The villagers of Oberammergau show us, as the sons of Asaph did, that such an enduring legacy can and does happen. As long as the baton is faithfully passed on, it matters not how many hands or how many years—the legacy lives on.

ASAPH
For Reflection and Discussion

1.   Who is Asaph? What is remarkable about his name in the historical records of Israel?

2.   What was the legacy Asaph left behind? Why do you think it lasted down the generations for 400 years?

3.   What part did music play in the preservation of Asaph's legacy? How can music help us today to package and deliver our legacy?

4.   Why is it important for a lasting legacy to begin in the home? Share about the kind of traditions, stories and memories you are creating with your family to pass on to the next generation.

5.   What can we do as a church to ensure that our faith is cherished and passed on to the next generation, and beyond?

Chapter Five

David
Do We Serve Only Our Generation?

In 1976 the Chinese Premier Zhou Enlai lay sick and debilitated in hospital. Meanwhile, the Communist Party Chairman Mao Zedong had succumbed to Parkinson's disease. While the Chinese had long revered aged leaders, the prospect of their two foremost leaders in such desperate conditions raised succession jitters. Mao passed away in September that year, and three potential contenders vied to fill the vacuum: Mao's wife Jiang Qing, the appointed heir Hua Guofeng, and a band of military generals led by diminutive Deng Xiaoping.

The account of how Deng eventually took over the Chinese leadership underlines the complex power politics in many succession stories. With lightning speed, the second and the third contenders acted together against the first. Less than a month after Mao's death, his widow and members of the Gang of Four were arrested and imprisoned. Hua, already Prime Minister, took over as Party Chairman, claiming the words of his predecessor, "With you in charge, I am at ease." However, the military leaders rallied around Deng, and within a year in between Party congresses, the table had been turned around.

It would take another four years before Hua was relieved of his office in 1982, and Deng positioned as the unquestioned leader of China. That was not the end of the succession process. In a mopping up operation, Deng dealt with the residue of supporters of Jiang and Hua. He called for a "retirement program" for Party cadres most of whom were 60 and older. By 1986, 1.8 million old cadres or 70% of the old guards were taken off the Party membership. Concurrently, a "rejuvenation policy" brought in fresh blood with younger cadres in support of China's modernisation. It had taken a decade for the succession to close the chapter on Mao.[117]

Such interplay of power and intrigue, schemes and manoeuvres, presents itself in many succession narratives, including those in the Bible. Few could match the turbulent events surrounding the transition from King David to King Solomon. Did David have a succession plan? Did he think of the generation after him, or did he think only to serve his own generation? Long after King David had come and gone, the apostle Paul declared, "…David, after he had served the purpose of God in his own generation, fell asleep and was laid with his fathers…."[118] John Edmund Haggai picked up the thought with this robust comment:

> "David served his generation. He could not serve the preceding generation. Only Christ could do that, for He is without beginning of days. David could not serve the subsequent generation. Only Christ can do that, for He is without end of years. You can no more serve the next generation than you can serve the last generation.
>
> "…More people get hung up on the spurious idea they can serve the next generation. Curtis Meadows of the huge Meadows Foundation of Dallas, Texas, said to a group of wealthy philanthropists, "I know of no foundation, where the will of the original grantor was carried out in the third generation. And that includes ours."[119]

That is true. We can think of institutions founded by men and women of deep biblical convictions which today promote and pursue secular ideals. Such benefactors who sought to serve the future generations must be turning in their graves. While this may be so, is it true that David thought only of his time and served only his generation? Perhaps a further reading of the chronicles of David's life is needed to answer that question.

GROUNDWORK FOR THE NEXT GENERATION

Firstly, consider his desire to build a temple for the LORD: "Behold, I dwell in a house of cedar, but the ark of the covenant of the LORD is under a tent."[120] His close confidant, Nathan, understood what David meant: the incongruity of the king in a grand palace and God's ark in a makeshift tent. He urged David to do what was in his heart. But as it turned out, God had other plans. David would not build a house for God; instead God would build a house for David:

> But that same night the word of the LORD came to Nathan, "Go and tell my servant David, 'Thus says the LORD: It is not you who will build me a house to dwell in…. Moreover, I declare to you that the LORD will build you a house.'"[121]

God reminded David of his past generations, how they wandered in the wilderness, and of his own generation, how he rose from a boy watching sheep to a monarch reigning over his people. Then God spoke of the next generation, how a son would arise after him to build a house for God: "When your days are fulfilled to walk with your fathers, I will raise up your offspring after you, one of your own sons, and I will establish his kingdom. He shall build a house for me, and I will establish his throne forever."[122] The privilege of building God's house would not be David's; it would pass on to his son.

Secondly, consider David's desire to help build a temple for the LORD. When told in no uncertain terms that the temple would not be built in his time or by him, he did not sulk, protest or wash his hands off the whole idea. Instead, he began to put in place dressed stones, supplies of iron for nails, cedar for timber, and bronze "in quantities beyond weighing" as well as the considerable manpower needed for the mammoth project.[123] David's heart pulsated with praise for God, and concern for his son.

> "Then King David went in and sat before the LORD and said, 'Who am I, O LORD God, and what is my house, that you have brought me thus far? And this was a small thing in your eyes, O God. You have also spoken of your servant's house for a great while to come, and have shown me future generations, O LORD God!'"[124]

> "For David said, 'Solomon my son is young and inexperienced, and the house that is to be built for the LORD must be exceedingly magnificent, of fame and glory throughout all lands. I will therefore make preparation for it.' So David provided materials in great quantity before his death."[125]

God had shown David a vision of his future generations: a son succeeding him, a temple built by his son, and a throne established by God "forever." These thoughts must have thrilled David to no end as he entertained, perhaps for the first time, the notion of succession.

A KING WHO COULD NOT KEEP WARM

But that is where the good part of the story ends. While the First Book of Chronicles presents us with an apparently smooth succession, the First Book of Kings fills us in with details of hidden flaws, high drama and close calls.[126] As in any succession, the inner workings are more complicated than what meets the eye. God does not hide from us the failings of men and women, for his sovereign purpose shines best against the darkness of human hearts.

In his masterly study of David's life, Eugene Peterson notes that there is not a single miracle in the story of David.

"Not one. There's never any question but that God is at the center of the plot and always present (although usually silent and hidden) in the details. But this is a story that never bypasses the ordinary, the everyday. David's humanity provides material that's worked on from the inside—quietly, insistently, hiddenly. The David story is a plunge into the earthiness of our humanity."[126a]

As David drew close to the end of his life, he cut a pitiful figure. The author of I Kings paints the shadow of a man, so feeble he could hardly keep warm, despite the pile of blankets heaped upon him. His servants recalled how their king had loved women, especially the young ones, and brought a teenage virgin to lie with him. Did they think that by physical intimacy and sexual arousal the fire of his youth could be rekindled? One commentator scoffs at such a move:

"They foolishly prescribed nuptials to one that should rather have been preparing for his funeral; but they knew what would gratify their own corruptions, and perhaps were too willing to gratify his, under colour of consulting his health. His prophets should have been consulted as well as his physicians in an affair of this nature."[127]

How true! Prophets should have been consulted, especially Nathan, the wise mentor and loyal friend of David. In the end it was Nathan who saved the day. Solomon did not stand next in line to the throne. There were six others before him, all born in Hebron, each by a different mother. Amnon had been murdered, Absalom had been killed, and Adonijah left evidently the oldest surviving son.[128] He made a bid for the throne by conspiring with Joab the army chief and Abiathar the priest to hold a lavish feast during which he would proclaim himself king. All his siblings except for Solomon had been invited. Had his scheme succeeded, the lives of both Solomon and his mother Bathsheba would be in grave danger.

Nathan moved into action with his own plan. He enlisted the help of Bathsheba to remind the king of his promise to make Solomon king. As she was speaking, Nathan made his entrance and reinforced the point. Learning for the first time what Adonijah was doing, David finally realised what was at stake. He roused from his senile stupor, collected his political wits, and ordered steps to ensure Solomon be recognised the rightful king. His personal mule would bear Solomon to the people with his royal endorsement, Nathan the prophet and Zadok the priest would represent the divine approval while Benaiah, head of David's elite guard, would underscore the military support.

The supporters of Adonijah, on hearing the news, abandoned their leader. The conspirators found themselves at the mercy of their new king who dealt with each of them subsequently. Though all ended well with Solomon firmly on the throne, we are left with a few troubling questions. What gave Adonijah the audacity to do what he did? How was he able to persuade the king's top military and religious leaders to join him? Did David ever make known his choice of Solomon as his successor? Obviously, many cracks appeared in David's succession plan, if he had one.

SECRETS, GRIEVANCES AND UNFINISHED TASKS

David presents us with a paradox when we consider his thoughts about succession. On the one hand, he made extravagant provisions for Solomon to build the temple. On the other hand, he made no provision for him to ascend the throne—that is, not till another claimant came along. What lessons can we learn from a transition that almost ended in disaster?

Firstly, note how David had to be reminded of his promise to make Solomon king. Leaders of organisations, especially of non-profit bodies, serve out of altruistic motives. Perhaps, for this reason, they draw immense fulfilment from their service. Could this also be the reason why they are often reticent to talk about succession? As the leader approaches retirement age, the responsibility falls on the board to initiate discussion about succession. Business organisations, unlike their non-profit counterparts, provide clear procedures for retirement, with steps for executive search and leadership transition. They consider the interests of the corporation over those of the individual. Could this be the reason why secular boards are more proactive about succession?

Discourse about succession often hits a personal raw nerve. The prospect of a successor taking over makes the incumbent feel redundant and insecure. The leader withdraws into denial. Perhaps, that was what happened to David. When Bathsheba and Nathan appeared before him, they plied him with information which betrayed his ignorance and amnesia. Did he not know that Adonijah had made himself king? Had he forgotten that Solomon was to be king? From all appearances, David had grown too detached from reality and too weak to rule. Yet, he had not taken the necessary steps to hand over his power.

David's tardiness in proclaiming Solomon king could be symptomatic of his neglect of the affairs of the kingdom. A king who could not keep himself warm could hardly keep the kingdom in shape. David's glory days had passed, and his declining faculties gave Adonijah the audacity to make himself king whether his father liked it or not. It also explained how even David's long-time loyalists Joab and Abiathar decided to jump ship. If David had placed the future of the kingdom above what was left of his own future, he would have taken the very steps he took when reminded by Bathsheba and Nathan. Succession planning means we subsume our personal interests to those of the larger body. Otherwise, we will end up with a leader unable to rule and reluctant to let another take the reins.

Secondly, note how David prepared materials for the temple, but failed to prepare his son for kingship. True, we have on record David's lengthy exhortations to Solomon about following the LORD and building the temple, but we see no follow-up to those words.

Evidently, David did not provide a role model for Solomon—or any of his sons. One son had raped his half-sister. Another had murdered a brother in cold blood, and then sought to usurp the throne. Adonijah merely followed in the footsteps of his siblings in a tragically dysfunctional family. Though he expressed his ambition to be king, openly and blatantly, David neither chided nor stopped him.[129]

David's relationship with each of his sons makes a depressing study in father-son relationship.[130] Since his one-night fling with Bathsheba, illicit sex and cold-blooded murder had plagued the family, and David had no moral ground to stand upon to rebuke his sons. We would have thought that things could be different for Solomon. As far as we know, he remained a filial son, his maturity acknowledged by David when he gave the final charge: "…You are a wise man. You will know what you ought to do…."[131]

Thanks to the intervention of Nathan, Solomon became co-regent with his father. The interregnum, brief though it was, gave us a glimpse into what David's relationship could have been with his sons. His death-bed charge to Solomon, a mix of sound spiritual counsel and shrewd political advice, tracked David's chequered life with its secrets, grievances and unfinished tasks.[132] Unfortunately, Solomon's mother enjoyed no such reprieve. As the favourite wife, she had to endure the sight of her husband lying with a girl young enough to be her granddaughter. If David needed someone to keep himself warm, why did he not ask for Bathsheba?

OPPORTUNITY COST

The zeal with which David prepared for the building of the temple was not matched by his concern for the grooming of his successor. Such neglect was not unusual, and in one case, cost half a million lives. King Charles II (1661-1700) ruled Spain and her far-flung empire from Mexico to the Philippines. He died without grooming any successor. Not known for his clarity of thought or soundness of judgement, he bequeathed his property to Philip who happened to be the grandson of his half-sister and King Louis XIV of France. Those who managed the succession unwittingly made Philip king of Spain. That put him in the line of succession to the French throne! The horror of a power bloc like Spain coming under France provoked a coalition of powers against the idea.

In 1701, the year after Charles II died, war broke out among opposing powers on the European continent. England, Portugal and the Dutch Republic, as well as other smaller states, joined in the fray. Spain, divided within herself, fell into civil war. The conflict spread to colonies in the West Indies, North and South America. Known as the *War of the Spanish Succession*, it lasted 13 years and claimed half a million lives. King Charles II went down in history as the one responsible for the War—all because he failed to put in place a viable succession plan.[133]

Not only did David fail to make succession a priority, he failed in his commitment to his family. So it is with many leaders today who excel in their vocational life but fall short in their personal and family life. The two spheres, work and family, cannot be totally separated; what happens in one affects the other. For David, his inability to manage his family impaired his competence to govern the nation.[134] This became painfully obvious when the kingdom almost came to ruin as a result of tensions within the family.

Could David have managed the succession better? Based on what is noted above, he could have done two things. One, he could have named his successor so that his subjects and other claimants to the throne would be left in no doubt. That would have put Adonijah in his place. That would also prepare Solomon to assume the throne. Two, David could have appointed Solomon king earlier and ruled with him as co-regents. Such a practice is not unknown in ancient times.[135]

That would have prepared the way for a seamless transition. But, as we have seen, such forethought and forward planning are best done, not by the leader who is stepping down, but by those around him.

PUSH AND SHOVE OF LIFE

Finally, note how human and divine intervention rescued David from the consequences of his inept handling of family and state affairs. What if Nathan had not known about the plot of Adonijah? What if Zadok and Benaiah had switched loyalties, like Joab and Abiathar, and joined the conspiracy? What if David, on hearing about the plot, had sunk so low in dementia that he could not rise to the occasion? In the final analysis, we see God's hand at work, over-ruling both the faults of David and the schemes of Adonijah.

In the pivotal scene of David's succession, with a touch of irony, God brought together the two characters who shared the secret of David's sin, Bathsheba and Nathan. They who knew how far he had fallen would intervene to help him stay the course and finish well. Reflecting on these events, commentator Gene Rice sums up:

> "The major theological point… is that God is present in the complex and ambiguous circumstances surrounding the succession of Solomon. Indeed, in spite of these circumstances, God's will was realized. This passage [I Kings 1] is no brief for withdrawal from hard choices, nor does it countenance letting the complexity and ambiguity of a situation paralyze one into inaction.

> "The chapter is a summons to the man or woman of God to be in the midst of the rowdy, untidy push and shove of human striving where God's purposes are at stake and to act with the boldness and astuteness of a Nathan. Bad leadership and evil can succeed only with the consent of the righteous."[136]

So David served the purpose of God in his own generation. No doubt, he prepared for the generation after him, but only in a limited sense. His desire to build the temple would be fulfilled by his son, but David could take no credit for the succession secured by others more alert and astute than he. The real hero was Nathan who, as a prophet like Samuel who anointed Saul and David, acted to ensure that only the one of God's choice ascended the throne.

DAVID
For Reflection and Discussion

1.   When King David was told he could not build the temple, what did he do? How did he serve God in his own generation? How did he serve God in his son's generation?

2.   While David made extensive preparations for the construction of the temple, he did not seem to have prepared his son for the throne. Why do you think he prepared so well for one but not for the other?

3.   David had to be reminded to declare Solomon king, and that only after Adonijah had declared himself king. Was it his ill health and memory loss due to age—or more?

4.   Describe the family life of David. How did the state of his family affect the affairs of his kingdom? Discuss how family life can help or hurt our work and service outside the home.

5.   At the crisis point of succession, the prophet Nathan saved the day. Despite human strife, intrigue and weakness, God still reigns sovereign. How should this assure us in the midst of the "push and shove" of life?

Chapter Six

Solomon
Why Is A Successful Transition So Hard To Repeat?

Alexander of Macedonia saw it coming. He had wanted to see the swamp of Babylonia. Together with some friends, they had set off in boats. As his boat navigated a narrow channel overgrown with overhanging reeds, his diadem got caught in them and fell into the water. One of the oarsmen jumped in and swam after it. He found it, and needing both hands to swim back to the boat, placed the diadem on his head. Though Alexander regained what he lost, he saw what happened as a bad omen.

Soon after, some unmixed wine he drank threw him into a violent frenzy. For days, he lay in pain. Then, knowing that his end was drawing near, he removed his ring and handed it to Perdiccas, one of his friends. With his dying breath, he asked that his kingdom be given only to the best and the strongest. Diodorus Siculus, the Roman historian writing in the first century AD, tells us that another friend, Craterus, "received instructions which the king had given him for execution; nevertheless, after the death of Alexander, it seemed best to the successors not to carry out these plans."[137]

Thus, Alexander the Great joined the ranks of many eminent leaders down the ages who failed to put success in succession. From antiquity, the challenge has been passing the baton without dropping it. Even Solomon in all his wisdom lamented,

"I hated all my toil in which I toil under the sun, seeing that I must leave it to the man who will come after me, and who knows whether he will be wise or a fool? Yet he will be master of all for which I toiled and used my wisdom under the sun. This also is vanity."[138]

Unlike Alexander's successor, Solomon took the words of his predecessor seriously. But as predecessor, Solomon would find his lament prophetic as his successor squandered all that he had left behind. We look at both ends of Solomon's life: how he received the legacy from his father, David, and what he left behind for his son, Rehoboam.

As a filial son, Solomon took to heart the last words of his father. Two names David mentioned in his dying moments lingered in Solomon's mind: Joab and Shimei. Recent events added two other names: Adonijah and Abiathar. Unless Solomon resolved outstanding issues with these individuals, his succession as king remained insecure. Joab and Abiathar had betrayed David by joining Adonijah in a bid for the throne. Shimei had cursed David when his throne was usurped by Absalom. Solomon's concern about these men seemed different from his father's. David spoke about what they did in the past; Solomon worried about what they would do in the future.

Joab, while serving David, had killed two army commanders, Abner and Amasa, "avenging in time of peace for blood that had been shed in war, and putting the blood of war on the belt around his waist and on the sandals on his feet." Shimei had cursed David with "a grievous curse" when he was fleeing from Absalom.[139] As to the fate of each of them, David told Solomon what to do without telling him how to do it.

"Act therefore according to your wisdom, but do not let his [Joab's] gray head go down to Sheol in peace... Now therefore do not hold him [Shimei] guiltless, for you are a wise man. You will know what you ought to do to him, and you shall bring his gray head down with blood to Sheol."[140]

Solomon acted accordingly: he ordered Joab's execution and Shimei's confinement within the city of Jerusalem. Joab tried to escape death by clinging to the horns of the altar, thinking perhaps that his executioner would not shed blood in a holy place. Shimei breached his detention, thinking he had not breached its terms. Both met their fateful end.[141] Thus Solomon eliminated the threat from two men of questionable loyalty who had acted in the past against their king.

David had left no instructions concerning Abiathar and Adonijah, but Solomon saw them as a threat too. He stripped Abiathar of his position as priest and banished him to his home village. When Adonijah asked for the Shunnamite concubine of David, Solomon confirmed his suspicion and ordered his death.[142] Only when Joab and Shimei, Abiathar and Adonijah were put away are we finally assured: "So the kingdom was established in the hand of Solomon."[143]

BLOODGUILT AND CURSE

Questions have been raised over the last instructions of David and the subsequent actions of Solomon. One commentator said of Solomon: "Ruthlessness mars his early days as king, to modern eyes; but he may well have noted the dire results of David's leniency...."[144] David might have been lenient, but could he also have been spiteful and vengeful? He placed on Joab the bloodguilt of two deaths, but was there more to David's fear of his otherwise loyal henchman? Joab was the only other person, apart from Bathsheba and Nathan, who was privy to David's heinous acts of adultery and murder. Did David fear that Joab might use that privileged information to undo Solomon's succession to the throne?

As for Shimei, David's initial reaction to his cursing was subdued. He refused to retaliate; instead he told his men, "Leave him alone, and let him curse, for the LORD has told him to. It may be that the LORD will look on the wrong done to me, and that the LORD will repay me with good for his cursing today."[145] Subsequently, Shimei apologised and David vowed by the Lord not to harm him.[146] What changed David's mind? He probably feared that Shimei, coming from the tribe of Saul, could revive the age-old Saul vs. David rivalry and challenge Solomon's kingship.

David's final advice to Solomon appeared to be an articulation of personal grievance mixed with genuine concern for his son. Could it be more the former than the latter, since no mention was made of Abiathar or Adonijah who also posed a threat? Some commentators point to the ancient concepts of bloodguilt and curses to explain David's insistence on justice for Joab and Shimei.[147] The Gibeonites, for example, demanded justice in the reign of David for bloodguilt against the house of Saul. Only when Saul's past crimes received their due penalty was justice satisfied and an old chapter closed.[148] Also, it was believed that a curse, if not dealt with, could take on a life of its own and haunt a future generation.

The success of Solomon's ascension to the throne depended on how promptly, decisively and wisely he closed past chapters. Perhaps, Solomon saw the unhappy chain of open-ended closures in his father's life: his silence over Amnon's rape of Tamar, his unforgiveness towards Absalom's murder of Amnon, his indulgence over Adonijah's illusions of grandeur. Much of his father's grief stemmed from such ambivalence, and Solomon chose not to go down that path. His execution of three men (two of them only after warning notices) and the banishment of a fourth would compare favourably with rulers who secured their power through the wholesale slaughter of family members, rival tribes, and opponents, real or imagined.

So far, so good. Solomon's succession to the throne had proceeded smoothly, with threats surmounted like speed bumps along the road. The bumpy ride in the early years soon gave way to a heady cruise into the future where the glorious kingdom envisioned by David unfolded. Solomon saw himself as "a little child" facing "a great people" and felt inadequate. He asked God for wisdom.

> "And now, O LORD my God, you have made your servant king in place of David my father, although I am but a little child. I do not know how to go out or come in. And your servant is in the midst of your people whom you have chosen, a great people, too many to be numbered or counted for multitude. Give your servant therefore an understanding mind to govern your people, that I may discern between good and evil, for who is able to govern this your great people?"[149]

Wisdom was given, and with it, wealth, honour and long life. In time, Solomon basked in the glow of success, sank into the lap of luxury, and soaked in the glamour of celebrity status. But success often sows the seeds of decay and ruin. Solomon's rise in power, followed by the building of the temple and the palace, bolstered by the fame of his wealth and wisdom, led to his apostasy from God. Ignoring injunctions in the Law of Moses, Solomon acquired horses and chariots in excess, as well as wives and concubines with their foreign gods. To build his lavish palace and to support his extravagant lifestyle, he imposed forced labour and heavy taxation. The subtle shift in the king's priorities is seen in the length of time he spent on his two major building projects: seven years on the temple, and 13 years on his palace.[150]

HEROES AND LOVE-HATE TRIANGLES

Signs of trouble for Solomon emerged in the form of three dissenters: Hadad the Edomite, Rezon of Damascus, and Jeroboam the Ephraimite.[151] Each was an adversary raised by God to challenge Solomon because of his disregard for divine parameters. While he was able to deal with men like Joab and Adonijah, and quickly put them away, he could not do the same with Hadad, Rezon and Jeroboam.

Hadad escaped the slaughter of his people, the Edomites, by David and Joab, and found his way as a royal infant into Egypt. He grew up there and found favour with the Pharaoh, married his sister, had a son raised in Pharaoh's family. When he heard that David and Joab had died, he asked Pharaoh for permission to return to Edom. Rezon too escaped the military campaign of David, became an outlaw, drawing to himself a band of marauders, and eventually leading them as the king of Damascus. Both Hadad and Rezon harassed Solomon throughout his reign.

The lives of these two men parallel those of Israel's heroes. Moses escaped the slaughter of the infants in Egypt and found his way into the family of the Pharaoh. David escaped the murderous attempts of Saul and became an outlaw with his band of followers.[152] The accounts of Hadad and Rezon inject into the narrative an underlying divine irony. God spared two men from death at the hand of David that they might return to haunt Solomon. The blessings God promised to David and his successors came with conditions: if Solomon failed to walk in God's ways, his throne would be shaken. The insurgencies by Hadad and Rezon were tremors in advance of a major quake.

With Hadad and Rezon presented as types of Moses and David, Solomon assumed the identity of a cross between Saul and the Pharaoh—not a flattering portrayal, but true nonetheless. As Saul, he was no longer a man after God's own heart.[153] As Pharaoh, he was no longer a king who cared about his people's hardship and suffering. Judgment on the kingdom and deliverance of the people would come next. So we are introduced to the third dissenter: Jeroboam.

Jeroboam began his career as one favoured by Solomon for his industry and ability. A wealthy landowner and capable military officer, he was commissioned to oversee the forced labour of the house of Joseph, representing major tribes in the north. Evidently, he became disillusioned with the king's oppressive rule, fomented a rebellion, and fled to Egypt for refuge.[154] One day, out alone in the countryside,

Jeroboam met Ahijah, a prophet, who delivered a show-and-tell prophecy. Taking the new set of clothes he was wearing, he tore it into 12 pieces, and offered Jeroboam 10 pieces. Then in no uncertain terms, Ahijah told him he would rival Solomon's successor, wrest 10 tribes from him and rule over them as king.[155] Thus Jeroboam would become Solomon's nemesis, in life and in death.

The parallels between them become even more intriguing when we place the names of key players in a sort of triangle: David-Saul-Samuel and Jeroboam-Solomon-Ahijah. David once found favour with Saul who then sought to kill him. Jeroboam too found favour with Solomon who then sought his life. Two prophets, Samuel and Ahijah, both from the same town of Shiloh, spoke of a kingdom being torn apart and given to another. David would be king after Saul, just as Jeroboam would be king after Solomon.

THE HARDLINE TOWARDS DOUBLE TRAGEDY

The glorious succession plan promised by God to David for his son and descendants no longer held water. Terms had been violated and conditions spurned. Solomon had to accept full responsibility for the dreadful state of affairs. When he succeeded David, he had sought to avoid the mistakes his father made. In the early stage of his reign, he closed unfinished chapters and tied up the loose ends. But decades into his rule, he forgot the words of his father to walk in the ways of God; he would leave a legacy of frayed threads for his son. Unfortunately, Rehoboam would not have the wisdom to handle what he inherited.

Rehoboam's succession paints a night-and-day contrast with Solomon's succession. One was handled with wisdom, the other with foolhardiness. One showed restraint, the other belligerence. To his credit, the new king began well by consulting the people, the older leaders and the younger ones. Each of them offered their counsel:

The People: "Your father made our yoke heavy. Now therefore lighten the hard service of your father and his heavy yoke on us, and we will serve you."

The Older Leaders: "If you will be a servant to this people today and serve them, and speak good words to them when you answer them, then they will be your servants forever."

The Younger Leaders: "Thus… shall you say to them, 'My little finger is thicker than my father's thighs. And now, whereas my father laid on you a heavy yoke, I will add to your yoke. My father disciplined you with whips, but I will discipline you with scorpions.'"[156]

In his folly, Rehoboam chose the advice of "the young men who had grown up with him." One wonders about the kind of generation produced by the 40-year reign of Solomon. But should we be surprised if the son—together with his peers—had taken after the father? They could not see what the common people saw, neither did they heed what the older generation advocated. While Solomon had been oblivious to popular sentiments, those who served him seemed more in touch with the populace. But Rehoboam, sheltered in the palace, distanced from the masses, pampered and spoilt, thought only of privileges and entitlements and the status quo.

He chose the hard line—in grasping, he lost his grip. The fruit was ripe for picking as Jeroboam stepped in and took 10 of the 12 tribes away from Rehoboam. Thus the kingdom, united under David and fortified under Solomon, felt apart under Rehoboam. But that was not the only tragedy. In our consideration of parallels between Rehoboam and Jerobaom, we saw how Jeroboam played the role of David taking the kingdom from Saul. Would history repeat itself, with a second David rescuing a faltering kingdom, and making it great again? That was not to be.

As king of the northern tribes, Jeroboam set up high places for idolatrous worship, recruited priests from outside the tribe of Levi, changed the religious calendar, and opened the way for the Canaanite Baal cult into Israel.[157] He would go down in history as such an evil king that every future bad king would be benchmarked against him with this refrain, "For he walked in all the way of Jeroboam the son of Nebat, and in the sins that he made Israel to sin, provoking the LORD, the God of Israel, to anger by their idols."[158] Thus the story of Solomon ends with a double tragedy: Rehoboam who fractured a kingdom and Jeroboam who corrupted it. Both missed the opportunity as successors to reap the bountiful blessings promised by God.

WEARING OUT A SOUL

The study of Solomon as both successor (of David) and predecessor (of Rehoboam) raises sobering questions about succession. Why is it so hard for a legacy to reach the third generation? Solomon received from his father what he could not pass on to his son. We have already seen a similar breakdown in transmission from Moses to the elders beyond Joshua. Why is a successful transition so difficult to replicate in the next generation?

Os Guinness writes about the "gravedigger's effect" by which we dig our own grave. We become successful in something which eventually becomes our downfall.[159] Solomon's wisdom brought him wealth which brought him wives and concubines which brought in foreign deities which brought Solomon down: "For when Solomon was old his wives turned away his heart after other gods, and his heart was not wholly true to the LORD his God, as was the heart of David his father."[160] The very things that made the kingdom great also brought the kingdom down.

As it happened with Solomon's kingdom, it could happen with anyone's family. Success in one generation brings along wealth which in turn brings down the next generation. Parents who have worked hard and succeeded to providing a better life for their children are understandably concerned if their children can handle what they inherit without working for it. Stories abound of children squabbling over property and money left behind for them. They inherit their parents' wealth without imbibing their fiscal prudence.

What is true of material inheritance may be true also of spiritual legacy. First-generation Christians often value their faith more than second-generation believers. This is especially so for those who had been persecuted by their family for their faith. They value what they believe, but their children growing in a faith-friendly environment may take it for granted and treat it lightly. In our succession story, David led a hard life and made it easier for Solomon who led an easy life and made it harder for Jeroboam. Such is the irony of the grave-digger's effect!

Solomon did well in taking over from David but did poorly in handing over to Rehoboam. Did he find it easier to succeed someone than to precede someone? One of the proverbs attributed to Solomon says, "Better is the end of a thing than its beginning, and the patient in spirit is better than the proud in spirit."[161] It is easy to start something but hard to finish it. Solomon started well but finished badly. Time is not always a friend, but an enemy. The long reign of Solomon provided time for what C.S. Lewis calls, "wearing out a soul by attrition." Speaking as a senior demon, he counsels a junior demon:

> "The long, dull monotonous years of middle-aged prosperity or middle-aged adversity are excellent campaigning weather... all this provides admirable opportunities of wearing out a soul by attrition... Prosperity knits a man to the World. He feels that he is *finding his place in it*, while really it is finding its place in him. His increasing reputation, his widening circle of acquaintances, his sense of importance, the growing pressure of absorbing

and agreeable work, build up in him a sense of really at home in earth which is just what we want."[162]

Success makes us feel so at home in the world that we forget our eternal destiny. Considering the natural course of time and human weakness, perpetuating a good succession is akin to swimming upstream. Unless we act counter-intuitively to deny self and obey God, we will be swept downstream. Ultimately, we are forced to take comfort in the sovereign hand of God in the affairs of succession. He is always one step ahead, raising someone to take over, to make a fresh start, and when all else fails, the son of David, the one greater than David, the Christ, comes to sit on the throne forever.

SOLOMON
For Reflection and Discussion

1.   How did Solomon demonstrate wisdom as he ascended the throne and dealt with the threats to his reign?

2.   What was his father's deathbed advice to him? Would you consider his words as spiteful and vengeful, lacking in grace and forgiveness? Why or why not?

3.   During Solomon's reign, adversaries rose against him, among them Hadad the Edomite and Rezon of Damascus. How did they resemble Israel's heroes, Moses and David, respectively? In what ways, did they make Solomon look like the Pharaoh of Egypt and King Saul?

4.   Compare the succession from David to Solomon, and Solomon to Rehoboam. How was Rehoboam foolish in the way he handled his succession? Was he really different from his father, or were they quite similar?

5.   What happened to Solomon during his long reign? Discuss how the soul of a person can be worn out by attrition. What can we do to take care of our soul?

Chapter Seven

Elijah
Can We Do Everything In One Lifetime?

What do we do when we feel overwhelmed by the weight of our responsibility? Where do we go when we are overtaken by the onslaught of life's challenges? John R. Mott, a Christian elder statesman of his time, counsels,

> "There is something in the vast expanses of the desert which sets the souls of men to brooding on the wide-ranging and eternal things.... It is worthwhile at frequent intervals to get away, into the woods, or mountains, or beside the ocean or on the edge of the great plains, and there to revise our petty and immediate concerns in the presence of nature, whose spaces are so vast and whose processes are so patient, so eternal."[163]

No wonder God answered Job's many questions by turning his attention to nature: "Where were you when I laid the foundations of the earth?"[164] By the same token, God addressed Elijah's despair by unleashing before him the forces of nature, then speaking to him in a whispered voice: "What are you doing here, Elijah?"[165] There, in the wilderness of Horeb, the prophet would revise his petty perspective in the light of God's space and time, vast and eternal. Indeed, Elijah would later travel across time with Moses to meet Jesus face to face.

The two men would confer with Jesus, talking about his *departure* from this world.[166] How appropriate: both Moses and Elijah died under extraordinary circumstances. Moses disappeared along a mountain path; Elijah vanished in the path of a fiery chariot—both their bodies were never found. The two prophets shared another distinction: each came to the brink of despair before they saw beyond their own short-sightedness to the divine big picture. Moses complained he could no longer bear the burden of leading the people. Elijah complained he could no longer carry the weight of the prophetic ministry:

> "It is enough; now, O LORD, take away my life, for I am no better than my fathers.... I have been very jealous for the LORD, the God of hosts. For the people of Israel have forsaken your covenant, thrown down your altars, and killed your prophets with the sword, and I, even I only, am left, and they seek my life, to take it away."[167]

Like Moses, Elijah felt abandoned and alone, believing he had to do it all by himself. God corrected his illusions. First, he told the prophet that he was not the only one left—there were 7,000 others who had not bowed to other gods. Second, God told Elijah to go and anoint another "to be prophet in your place."[168] As Moses found Joshua, so Elijah found Elisha. In each case, the successor did not immediately take over, but spent years learning under his master.

BRING PREDECESSOR BACK, DEAD OR ALIVE

Elijah anointed Elisha by throwing his mantle over him, a symbolic act signifying a transfer of authority from one to another. But the act meant more—as expressed in the German word *mantelkind*, literally *a child of the mantle*, or a spiritual son. Elijah took his protégé under his tutelage, and became a father to him. At the end of his life, Elisha would ask for "a double portion" of Elijah's spirit, reminiscent of the right of inheritance belonging to the eldest son.[169]

By then, schools of prophets had sprung up in significant cities, including Bethel, the centre of idolatrous cult worship. Elijah had raised many sons, but among them, none like Elisha. He was described as the prophet "who poured water on the hands of Elijah."[170] As an apprentice, Elisha washed the hands of his master before and after meals. The context suggests eminence since Elijah was held in high esteem, and a lowly servant of his would share in his prestige.

Elijah had come a long way from when he felt he was the only one. The schools of prophets, founded in the days of Samuel, now looked to him as their mentor. No wonder, when he felt his time was drawing to an end, he went on a final journey for one last visit to the schools. Accompanied by his protégé, Elijah must have viewed the prophets with a wry smile—to think at one time he prided himself as the only one! As he made his exit, he left with the assurance that others would take his place. But while he was ready to leave, his followers were not ready to see him leave. Like Moses, Elijah left without a trace. Like Moses' followers, Elijah's disciples insisted on a search for the body. They were not prepared to lose him.

> "And they said to him [Elisha], 'Behold now, there are with your servants fifty strong men. Please let them go and seek your master. It may be that the Spirit of the LORD has caught him up and cast him upon some mountain or into some valley.' And he said, 'You shall not send.' But when they urged him till he was ashamed, he said, 'Send.' They sent therefore fifty men. And for three days they sought him but did not find him."[171]

Such devotion by the predecessor's loyalists is understandable. Even Elisha was made to feel ashamed that he did not show such loyalty. Nevertheless, it is misdirected energy, and sometimes a serious impediment to a smooth succession. Instead of rallying around the successor, the loyalists long to have the predecessor back, alive or dead. Could God be sending a clear message to the people when he denied them even the body of their supreme leader to venerate? They had to let go and move on.

NOT IN ONE LIFETIME

Success in succession depends on the predecessor, the successor, and the people. Elijah the predecessor had come to terms with the limits of what he could do. His experience at Mount Horeb—where he asked to die—certainly convinced him that he could not do it alone. Consider the three assignments God gave him at that time:

> "And the LORD said to him, 'Go, return on your way to the wilderness of Damascus. And when you arrive, you shall anoint Hazael to be king over Syria. And Jehu the son of Nimshi you shall anoint to be king over Israel, and Elisha the son of Shaphat of Abel-meholah you shall anoint to be prophet in your place.'"[172]

Of the three assignments, Elijah could complete only one of them. He was to anoint Hazael to be king over Syria, and Jehu king over Israel. He never did. But he did anoint Elisha who was responsible for Hazael becoming king, while Elisha's servant was instrumental to Jehu becoming king.[173]

The servant of Elisha represents the third generation after Elijah. Not given a name, he is known to us simply as "one of the sons of the prophets," "the young man," and "the servant of the prophet."[174] Thus the three-fold mission committed to Elijah found its fulfillment across the generations. It could not be accomplished in one lifetime. The question as to whether Elijah failed in his obedience to God's commission need not arise: in his successor, Elijah accomplished it all. Delegating what we cannot do to someone who can do it is the beginning of a successful transition.

Leadership studies sometimes refer to a phenomenon associated with the banyan tree. Carson Pue, president of Arrow Leadership

Ministries, an international ministry committed to mentoring church leaders, conducts a workshop he entitles, "Nothing Grows Under the Banyan Tree." He explains:

> "The Banyan tree is a broad, spreading, dense tropical tree. The leaf canopy is so dense that rain is unable to penetrate—leaving the soil beneath barren of nutrients. I use this imagery to convey how many young leaders fail to grow under the canopy of existing leaders. They are starved of the essential nutrients required for growth."[175]

Younger leaders need nurture and space for growth. Older leaders need to dominate less and delegate more. Most of all, leaders need to give time to those under their care. Elijah and Elisha belonged to a blessed age where learning took place with teacher and student living and working together. Without high tech intervention, they settled for a high touch relationship. The relationship between Elijah and Elisha came to a climax in their final journey together through the cities of Gilgal, Bethel, Jericho, and on to the Jordan, retracing the steps of Joshua as Israel claimed the Promised Land.

In each place, a school of prophets represented a witness for those who still held true to the faith of their forefathers. When asked by his master to stay at each of the cities, Elisha declined; he was determined to follow Elijah to the end. Such was the warmth of devotion and bond of allegiance between successor and predecessor. Elijah nurtured Elisha, and paved the way for a successful transition.

WHISPER AFTER THUNDER

Success in transition also depends on the successor. Elisha apparently came from a well-to-do family. He was found ploughing with 12 yoke of oxen. We may safely assume the other 11 men were his father's servants. When Elisha chose to follow Elijah, he sealed his decision by slaughtering his yoke of oxen, burning his ploughing implements, and hosting a farewell banquet, no doubt serving the sacrificed animals to his family and guests for a sumptuous meal. His conviction was clear, and commitment absolute.

Yet, it would be a while before he wore his master's mantle entirely. He would watch his master take on King Ahab and his sons, Ahaziah and Jehoram, as the nation plunged further into idolatry and immorality. Perhaps the challenges he witnessed led him to ask Elijah for a double portion of his spirit. He might have thought his master's shoes too big for him, and asked for bigger feet to fill them. Did he really equal or surpass his master? One commentator considers Elisha "a very faint and feeble replica of Elijah"[176]—this would be true if we look only at the miracles both prophets performed. Elisha could not match his master's miracles in scope and spectacle. One was a soft whisper compared to the other's deafening thunder.

In the nature of succession, the successor often labours in the shadow of the predecessor, and seldom comes out of it. On a visit to Zurich, Switzerland, I was keen to learn all I could about Ulrich Zwingli, the Swiss reformer, a contemporary of Martin Luther, born only weeks apart. Standing before a cathedral in the city, I was introduced to Heinrich Bullinger, his statue in prominent relief on the front wall. Till then, I had never heard of that name.

In 1519, at the age of 15, Bullinger was sent by his father to Cologne to study for the ministry at a time when Luther had created no small stir with his "Ninety-Five Theses" against the church. Convinced that Luther was more faithful to the church fathers and Scriptures, Bullinger aborted his studies and returned home. In 1524, he contacted Zwingli and subsequently spent five months in Zurich. When Zwingli died in battle in 1531, Bullinger received a call to pastor his church in Zurich. When he stood in Zwingli's pulpit and preached, he "thundered a sermon from the pulpit that many thought Zwingli was not dead but resurrected like the phoenix." That same year, at the age of 27, he was elected the successor to Zwingli, an office he served till his death in 1575.[177]

FINAL PIECE OF PUZZLE

Little known as he is, Heinrich Bullinger qualifies as a "faint and feeble" impression of Zwingli—or does he? Successors build on their predecessors' work. If the latter had been ground-breaking, boundary-pushing and paradigm-shifting, it surely makes more waves and attracts more attention. The one who comes after to consolidate the work and ensure an enduring legacy, usually does not cut a high profile, though his contribution is as invaluable and essential. As Bullinger followed Zwingli, so Elisha came after Elijah—each accomplishing God's purpose in his own way, the successor continuing and completing what his predecessor started.

Take an example: Elijah pronounced a prophecy against King Ahab and his wife Jezebel. She had procured false witnesses against Naboth, the owner of a vineyard, and had him killed so that her husband could annex the land and add it to his adjacent palace grounds. Justice had been mocked, and the perpetrators of crimes rewarded. But Elijah made it clear to Ahab:

> "Thus says the LORD: 'In the place where dogs licked up the blood of Naboth shall dogs lick your own blood.'

> "And of Jezebel the LORD also said, 'The dogs shall eat Jezebel within the walls of Jezreel. Anyone belonging to Ahab who dies in the city the dogs shall eat, and anyone of his who dies in the open country the birds of the heavens shall eat.'" [178]

Elijah did not live to see the fulfillment of his prophecy. Elisha played a part which brought the death of Ahab at the hand of the king of Syria. The final piece of the puzzle involved a servant of Elisha who anointed Jehu king and set in motion the events that led to the ignominious death of Jezebel.[179] Thus the work of God—in bringing judgment upon the house of Ahab, and an end to the dynasty of Omri— was initiated by one, and completed by another, with yet another in between. That is what succession is about: a relay race, with several runners, each taking turn to grasp the one baton, running towards one goal. No one runner does it all; each plays a part to complete the whole.

When Elijah was whisked to heaven, Elisha cried, "My father, my father! The chariots of Israel and its horsemen!" Overcome with personal grief, having lost a father figure, he nevertheless declared the legacy of his master from what he saw in those final dramatic moments: Elijah had been to Israel as the thundering chariots and spirited horses—embodying true strength and courage for a tottering nation. Interestingly, at Elisha's death, without drama, the king of Israel would echo those same words to Elisha: "My father, my father! The chariots of Israel and its horsemen!"[180] Perhaps it took a lifetime for the disciple to fill the shoes of his master, and in the end, to share the same tribute.

It is said that the height of a tree is best seen when it is cut down. So is the greatness of a leader fully known when he is no longer around. However, as J. Oswald Sanders wisely observes:

> "...the removal of a leader cuts him down to size in relation to the work of God. However great his achievement, he is not irreplaceable. The time comes when his special contribution is not the need of the hour. The most gifted leader has limitations that become apparent only after the complimentary gifts of his successor cause the work to develop along lines for which the former leader was unfitted."[180a]

Finally, succession depends on the people. The predecessor may be willing to let go, the successor may be ready to take on, but what if the people refuse to accept the transition? When I decided to step down from the church I had pastored for almost 20 years, the people described the announcement in mixed metaphors: "a ton of bricks" hitting them like "a thunder-bolt." My wife and I had grown up in the church since our teenage years and younger, and the people took pride in me as their first and "home-grown" pastor.

Thankfully, my next appointment with a Christian organisation took me to another country. Yet the distance did not prevent well-intentioned friends asking me how long my term would be and when I would return to the church. Several years after I left, when the church went through some rough waters, I received pleas asking me to seriously and prayerfully consider returning. I knew then, as now, that it was not in the best interests of the church nor of my successor to even consider those requests. I prayed instead for my successor to succeed, for his failure would be mine as well.

DROPPING MANTLE AT EXIT

For any succession to work, the people need to be convinced that the leaders are serious about the process. Otherwise, they will be waiting to see the succession fall apart. Often, the one to convince the people is the predecessor. He can do so by consistently affirming the successor, resolutely refusing to interfere in his responsibilities, and graciously removing himself from the scene. The people will get the message in due time. Unfortunately, predecessors who have built strong bonds with their followers find it hard to do the above, and unwittingly become accomplices with the people in bringing down their successors.

Would the people have accepted Joshua if Moses was still alive, or Elisha if Elijah was still around? Considering the spiritual giants that these predecessors were, marked out by miraculous signs, and defining the generations they served, no succession could have worked unless God removed them in the way he did. The people were thus left with no choice but to look away from the past to the future, and to their new leader.

In the midst of a succession, people are understandably tentative and cautious. They need assurance from both predecessor and successor. In particular, the successor has to assure and convince the people of his worthiness. Elisha would establish his credibility when his miracles mirrored those of Elijah: the parting of River Jordan, the healing of bad water, the judgment upon the mocking juveniles, the provision for a widow, and the raising to life of a young boy.[181] The first miracle was perhaps the most important:

> "Then he took the cloak of Elijah that had fallen from him and struck the water, saying, 'Where is the LORD, the God of Elijah?' And when he had struck the water, the water was parted to the one side and to the other, and Elisha went over."[182]

With 50 men from the Jericho school of prophets as witnesses, and with his master's mantle in his hand, Elisha enacted what Elijah had done earlier on. He shouted the rhetorical question, "Where is the LORD, the God of Israel?" Surely, the LORD had not departed with Elijah. Later, when they returned to Jericho, the prophets would answer that question with an affirmation, "The spirit of Elijah rests on Elisha."[183] God was still with them.

American media, ruthless as they come, give their presidents the first 100 days in office to prove their mettle.[184] Most presidents need more time, but sooner or later, they must prove they deserve to be elected. John F. Kennedy resolved the Cuban missiles crisis which brought the world to the brink of a nuclear war. George W. Bush rallied the nation in the aftermath of terrorist attacks which took almost 3,000 lives on home soil. The first year in office has been dubbed the "honeymoon year" but many successors have found that it is anything but romantic. Reality soon sets in, expectations run high, and disappointments lurk round the corner.

Like Elisha, a successor needs to be convicted of his calling. The prophet refused to leave his master because he must see him when he made his final departure. Then only would he be certain that he was the one. It was as Elijah had told him, "…if you see me as I am being taken from you, it shall be so for you, but if you do not see me, it shall not be so."[185] Elisha saw it all, and left convinced beyond any doubt that he was indeed the anointed successor. Being thus convicted, he went on to serve the people with confidence and credibility.

To the end, predecessor and successor walked together, each believing that his time had come, one dropping his mantle, the other picking it up. As one exited, the other took his place, demonstrating that in God's economy, no one does it all. Each fulfills only a part of an enterprise which, like the world of nature, stretches far into the distance and wide across time.

ELIJAH
For Reflection and Discussion

1.   What did Elijah have in common with Moses? Why did Elijah feel that he had to do it all alone? How did God correct his thinking?

2.   What was unusual about the death of Elijah? Why did his followers want to go and look for his body? Is this still true today when people long to have their predecessor back with them?

3.   Of the three assignments given by God to Elijah, he could only complete one. Did Elijah fail in his mission? If not, why not?

4.   Elisha did not cut as impressive a figure as Elijah. Compare them with Zwingli and Bullinger. Why are successors not as well-known and remembered as their predecessors?

5.   How does the process of succession compare with the world of nature? Discuss the concluding statement about the predecessor and the successor: "Each fulfills only a part of an enterprise which, like the world of nature, stretches far into the distance and wide across time."

Chapter Eight

Hezekiah
How Could So Much Good Produce So Much Evil?

Proverbs describe life with all its ambiguity and complexity: "Good comes to better, and better to bad." "Out of a great evil often comes a great good." "Evil follows good, good follows evil."[186] Good and bad are mixed in life. Good can come out of a bad situation; likewise, evil can arise from a good situation. Such is sometimes the story of succession.

Sandwiched between two of the worst kings of Judah, Hezekiah provides an intriguing study in the succession of kings. How could a bad king like Ahaz produce a good king like Hezekiah? And how could a good king like Hezekiah produce a bad king like Manasseh? Consider how each king is described in the line of succession from father to grandson:

Ahaz, father: "...he did not do what was right in the eyes of the LORD, as his father David had done, but he walked in the ways of the kings of Israel."

Hezekiah, son: "...he did what was right in the eyes of the LORD, according to all that David his father had done."

Manasseh, grandson: "...he did what was evil in the sight

of the LORD, according to the abominations of the nations whom the LORD drove out before the people of Israel."[187]

When Hezekiah succeeded his father to the throne, he had seen the kingdom of Israel succumb to the Assyrian superpower. Hezekiah's kingdom, Judah, viewed Israel with mixed feelings. They were once one kingdom under Solomon till his foolish and reckless son ruptured it, alienating 10 of the 12 tribes to the north under a different king. Since then, Israel never saw a good king; every one without exception led the people downward in the path of idolatry and immorality.

In the year 722 BC, after the reigns of 21 kings, Israel was ripe for divine judgement. Assyrian armies marched towards its capital city, Samaria, and laid siege against it. After three years, as starvation, death and despair set in, the spirit of the people broke, and the city surrendered. Thus, the kingdom of Israel came to an ignominious end as royalty and commoners alike staggered into captivity in Assyria.

Hezekiah witnessed the demise of Israel in the early years of his reign. With Samaria only a stone's throw from his own capital city Jerusalem, the new king must have found the development too close for comfort. Perhaps Hezekiah reflected on the cause of Israel's downfall, and saw the hand of God against the nation whose kings had adopted pagan practices.[188] Perhaps Hezekiah reflected on the state of his own kingdom whose previous king, his father, had adopted similar pagan practices.

ABOUT-TURN AND ABOUT-FACE

Whatever the motivation, Hezekiah instituted sweeping reforms in Judah. Firstly, he restored the temple. The holy place, neglected for decades, had become a dumping ground for trash. It took more than two weeks just to haul away the garbage and clean up the place. Secondly, he restored worship. Hezekiah recalled the priests and

Levites, set them in their divisions and put them to work. Once again the songs of praise and smoke of sacrifices filled the temple.

Thirdly, he restored the Passover. Of all the festivals, this most clearly defined the people of God. It reminded them of their time as slaves in Egypt, their deliverance under Moses, and God's faithfulness as they journeyed through the wilderness and eventually settled in the Promised Land. Hezekiah even extended an invitation to the remnants of Israel to join in the celebration. In addition, he did what the kings before him had not done. He dismantled the high places of pagan worship, and smashed the bronze serpent from the time of Moses which had become an object of worship.

On the political front, Hezekiah faced a challenge from the Assyrians. His father Ahaz had made a treaty with the king of Assyria, an act of submission in return for protection. Hezekiah took a bold step and abrogated the treaty. Knowing that it amounted to a declaration of war against the arrogant superpower, he fortified Jerusalem, strengthening its walls, lining them with towers, and preparing weapons of war. To withstand a siege, he embarked on an engineering feat: the digging of a tunnel through 600 metres of solid rock to bring water from the Spring of Gihon into the city's Pool of Siloam.

Sure enough, the Assyrian king, Sennacherib, despatched his forces and captured all the fortified cities of Judah, and boasted that he had Hezekiah caged like a bird in Jerusalem. In desperation, and perhaps, from a lapse of faith in God, Hezekiah pleaded, "I have done wrong; withdraw from me. Whatever you impose on me I will bear."[189] In an about-face, the king emptied his palace and the temple of gold and silver—even stripping the gold that covered the doors and doorposts of the temple—and gave it all to Sennacherib. The humiliation cut Hezekiah to the bone, politically and spiritually. He had not only yielded to a pagan king, but had implied that his God had capitulated as well.

The Assyrian king, far from being appeased by the bounty of gold and silver, became emboldened by Hezekiah's admission of weakness. Going back on his word, he set up camp a mere 40 kilometres from Jerusalem and sent his field commander, Rabshakeh,[190] to deliver an ultimatum for Hezekiah to surrender. Rabshakeh insulted the envoys sent by Hezekiah, intimidated the people (speaking to them in their native language, Hebrew), and blasphemed the name of the God of Judah. Despite the air of conceit and condescension, the logic seemed irrefutable:

> Thus says Sennacherib king of Assyria, "On what are you trusting, that you endure the siege in Jerusalem? Is not Hezekiah misleading you, that he may give you over to die by famine and by thirst, when he tells you, 'The LORD our God will deliver us from the hand of the king of Assyria'? ...Do you not know what I and my fathers have done to all the peoples of other lands? Were the gods of the nations of those lands at all able to deliver their lands out of my hand?"[191]

The Assyrian king and his armies had laid waste the nations around Judah and the cities within it. Neither their kings nor their gods had been able to stop them. Hezekiah's faith was put to the severest test. What reckless risk had he taken by angering the pagan king? In reversing the foreign policy of his predecessor, had he pushed his kingdom over the brink to war and annihilation? Moreover, the domestic reforms he had instituted in Judah—would they make a difference to the fate of the nation? Could he still put his trust—and his people—unreservedly in the hand of his God? Israel to the north had fallen, and it looked like Judah would follow likewise.

NO STRENGTH AT CHILDBIRTH

The kings of Israel and Judah had long faced the double threat of political domination and religious infiltration. On the one hand, the power blocs of Egypt, Assyria and Babylonia had eyed the buffer strip of land and coveted its strategic location. On the other hand, the more immediate neighbours of the Canaanite tribal nations had enticed the people with their pagan gods and practices. Hezekiah had chosen to resist them both. What price would he pay for such a course of action?

With an imminent siege and the grim prospect of misery prolonged to certain defeat, Hezekiah tore his clothes, put on sackcloth and went to the temple to seek God. The anguished heart of Hezekiah may be seen in the message he sent to the prophet, Isaiah:

> "This day is a day of distress, of rebuke, and of disgrace; children have come to the point of birth, and there is no strength to bring them forth. It may be that the LORD your God heard all the words of the Rabshakeh, whom his master the king of Assyria has sent to mock the living God, and will rebuke the words that the LORD your God has heard; therefore lift up your prayer for the remnant that is left."[192]

The people, crying in distress, stung by rebuke, cowering in disgrace, had no one else to turn to, but to God. The metaphor of childbirth aptly summed up their predicament: pain, compounded by weakness, threatened by death. Hezekiah could well be describing himself. Perhaps, on hindsight, his futile offer of tribute turned on him as a rebuke for his weak faith. His father had during his time offered tribute to the king of Assyria, and succeeded in currying his favour. Ahaz had gone one step further: he had a replica of the Assyrian altar made and installed in the temple in Jerusalem.[193] Hezekiah would do no such thing.

Instead he sought the counsel of God's spokesman, Isaiah. In no uncertain terms, the prophet proclaimed the fate of the Assyrian king: "…he shall hear a rumor and return to his own land, and I will make him fall by the sword in his own land."[194] And so it happened: God routed the Assyrian army, the king returned home, and was subsequently assassinated by two of his own sons. The threats of Sennacherib and the insults of Rabshakeh fell away as empty words, giving way to Isaiah's words as prophecy fulfilled to the last detail.

UNTHINKING AND UNFEELING

At the time of national calamity, Hezekiah also faced a personal crisis. He fell ill, and Isaiah told him he would die. The king pleaded with God who promised to have his life extended by 15 years. That new lease of life would prove a stumbling block for Hezekiah. Firstly, a Babylonian delegation came to congratulate him on his recovery from illness, and his successful resistance against the Assyrians. The Babylonians represented a rising power to challenge the Assyrians, and Hezekiah wanted them on his side—not knowing that he was unwittingly exchanging dependence on God for dependence on man.

The conversation between Hezekiah and Isaiah following the Babylonian visit gives us insights into the subtle shift in Hezekiah's walk with the LORD.

Isaiah: "What did these men say? And from where did they come to you?"
Hezekiah: "They have come from a far country, from Babylon."

Isaiah: "What have they seen in your house?"
Hezekiah: "They have seen all that is in my house; there is nothing in my storehouses that I did not show them."

Isaiah: "Hear the word of the LORD: Behold, the days are coming, when all that is in your house, and that which your fathers have stored up till this day, shall be carried to Babylon. Nothing shall be left, says the LORD. And some of your own sons, who shall be born to you, shall be taken away, and they shall be eunuchs in the palace of the king of Babylon."

Hezekiah: "The word of the LORD that you have spoken is good."
Hezekiah (to himself): "Why not, if there will be peace and security in my days?"[195]

Hezekiah's pride got the better of him as he showed off his wealth to the foreign visitors. No doubt, the assets he had given away had been replaced by war booty from the Assyrians when they were routed. He was acting as if he was the champion by whose hand the victory had been won. He had forgotten how close he was to death—from war or from illness. The danger from the Assyrians might be past, but the threat from the Babylonians was still to come. Hezekiah had unknowingly tempted them with his riches, and received a veiled rebuke from Isaiah. In an unguarded moment, Hezekiah revealed the ambivalent condition of his heart, as a telling comment summing up his life would inform the reader:

"And so in the matter of the envoys of the princes of Babylon, who had been sent to him to inquire about the sign that had been done in the land, God left him to himself, in order to test him and to know all that was in his heart."[196]

Despite the sparing of his life, the heart of Hezekiah was found wanting when it was tested. The 15-year extension of Hezekiah's life would prove a stumbling block for another reason—as seen in the king's smug reply to Isaiah. When told that his kingdom would come to an end in the reigns of his sons, Hezekiah called it "good," comforting himself that it would not happen in his lifetime. Not only was he unthinking towards the Babylonian visitors, he was unfeeling towards his succeeding generation. His son and successor, Manasseh, would be born in those 15 years, and grow up to undo everything Hezekiah had done. The fact that Manasseh began his reign at the age of 12 meant he had no direct experience of his father's early reforms or his father's utter dependence upon God in the face of the Assyrian menace.

LAST THINGS FIRST

We can only guess at the kind of example the father was to him during the 12 years of Manasseh's life before he became king. How could such a good king produce a son whose kingship would rank as the worst among the kings of Judah? One clue may be found in Hezekiah's concern only for his generation. As long as he had peace during his watch, he did not care what happened next. Could this blinkered view of his reign have arisen from the knowledge that his life would end in so many years? Such knowledge could have led to one of two outcomes: to enjoy the most of the moment, or to prepare the best for the next.

Randy Pausch, a computer science professor at Carnegie Mellon University, was invited to deliver a lecture in the "Last Lecture Series"—so called because it gives learned dons an opportunity to distill their wisdom and share it as if it were their last word. The lecture took on new meaning for Pausch as he learned he had terminal pancreatic cancer. Titling his lecture, "Really Achieving Your Childhood Dreams," he revisited his own childhood and recalled dreams fulfilled. He then turned to his own children:

> "There are so many things I want to tell my children, and right now, they are too young to understand. Dylan just turned six. Logan is three. Chloe is eighteen months old. I want the kids to know who I am, what I've always believed in, and all the ways in which I've come to love them."[197]

We wonder if Hezekiah, knowing he had limited time with his children, ever sought to tell them who he was and what he believed in. Did he believe in putting last things first? Did he prepare his son Manasseh for his turn at the throne? Apparently not—or maybe he did. Manasseh, after a long 55-year reign, suffered a fate from which his father had been spared. The commanders of the Assyrian king captured Manasseh and brought him bound in chains to Babylon. The chronicler, in recording what happened, reminds us of the semblance of the father in the son:

> "And when he was in distress, he entreated the favor of the LORD his God and humbled himself greatly before the God of his fathers. He prayed to him, and God was moved by his entreaty and heard his plea and brought him again to Jerusalem into his kingdom. Then Manasseh knew that the LORD was God."[198]

By then, it was too little, too late. Judah, like Israel, had gone too far, and five turbulent decades separated Manasseh from the eventual downfall forecasted by Isaiah. Thus ended the long line of the kings of Judah among whom the triad of kings—Ahaz, Hezekiah and Manasseh—provides us with much food for thought.

Firstly, consider the strange paradox of godly children coming from ungodly homes, and vice versa. Hezekiah saw the bad example of his father, and chose a different path. Manasseh saw the good example of his father, and likewise chose differently. Such decisions confound us. Yet, when we consider children who have grown up in exemplary homes turning away from the faith of their parents, we realise that a godly home is no guarantee of godly children. Some parents, in forcing their faith upon their children, imposing upon them the form without modelling for them the essence, may actually drive their children from their faith. Eventually, only God knows how our children will turn out.

Our responsibility is not to speculate how they will turn out, but to provide a godly home for them to turn out well. Manasseh, despite his evil ways, may well illustrate the truth of the counsel, "Train up a child in the way he should go; even when he is old he will not depart from it."[199] As parents, we want to live with the assurance that, however our children turn out, we have done our part in raising them. If we have laid a strong foundation when they are young, we can live with the assurance that, however far they stray, they will find their way home one day. Even if, for some reason, they do not, we rest in the knowledge that we have discharged our stewardship of them.

POOR BARGAIN AND MISSED OPPORTUNITY

Secondly, consider the mixed blessing of an extended life. Sung Shang-Chieh from Fujian, China, saw a vision of Jesus who changed his name to John, called him to the ministry of John the Baptist, and told him he had 15 years to do it. He wasted no time, set aside a comfortable career, became an itinerant evangelist, and blazed a trail of revival in East Asia in the 1930s. Souls were saved, churches revived, and entire communities transformed. When he died at the age of 43, John Sung had brought hundreds of thousands of people to Christ.[200]

We do not sense the same urgency in Hezekiah's life. If anything, his remarkable recovery from illness and astounding success in repulsing the Assyrians made him complacent. He failed to use the "grace time" to extend his influence beyond his generation. Like many successful leaders, his success ended with him. Had Hezekiah died from his illness, Manasseh would not have been born, and the history of Judah could have been different. On hindsight, 55 years for a nation of the worst and longest rule by a king was a poor bargain for 15 years for Hezekiah.

"Those fifteen years would prove that God's wisdom far exceeds human wisdom. During those added years, Manasseh was born, and he eventually succeeded Hezekiah as king of Judah. Manasseh, who reigned for fifty-five years, was the most evil king ever to rule Judah…. He shed much innocent blood during his reign; every part of the nation suffered from his cruelty. All these hardships were caused by Manasseh, a king who would never have been born if Hezekiah had accepted God's will for his life!"[201]

Finally, consider the tragedy of missed opportunity. When God told Hezekiah to put his house in order before his imminent death, he begged for mercy on account of the good he had done.[202] God gave him a 15-year reprieve, doubling his eventual 29-year reign. Yet, Hezekiah failed to set his house in order or prepare for his postponed death. It reminds us of the Peanuts cartoon strip of Charlie Brown sitting in a class praying desperately for the bell to ring before he would be asked about his unfinished homework. The bell rang in time for him to heave a sigh of relief and rush out of class. "Are you going to do your homework now?" his friend Lucy asked. "Homework?" Charlie said with his characteristic grin, "I'm going to play ball!"

Hezekiah had 15 years and he squandered it. No one else in the Bible, except for Jesus, knew exactly when he was going to die. We can imagine Hezekiah counting down the years. Did he set in place people and practices to ensure that his reforms would last into the next generation? Or did he simply assume they would? With a successor barely a teenager, what precautions did Hezekiah take to ensure that his son would cherish and continue his legacy? Apparently little, or none.

Hezekiah took the best of himself and his reign to his grave, allowing the worst in his son and successor to wreak havoc upon the next generation. Tragically, Hezekiah represents predecessors who neglect to prepare for their exit. They fail to take responsibility for writing life's next chapter. They take their success with them and leave their successors to undo what they have done.

HEZEKIAH
For Reflection and Discussion

1.   How was Hezekiah different from his father? What led him to institute radical changes to his father's policies concerning religion and politics?

2.   How did the Assyrian king respond to Hezekiah's sweeping reforms which included the abrogation of a treaty with the Assyrians? How did Hezekiah try to appease the Assyrian threat? Did it work?

3.   While his kingdom was at risk, Hezekiah faces a personal crisis with his health. Imagine you were in his shoes, and share your thoughts and feelings, especially when you are told you would die soon.

4.   God delivered Hezekiah from the Assyrians and from death. What was his attitude when each of the crises was past? What did he do with the additional 15 years God added to his life?

5.   "Hezekiah took the best of himself and his reign to his grave, allowing the worst in his son and successor to wreak havoc upon the next generation." Consider how this could happen to us today when we neglect our walk with the Lord and our responsibility to our family.

Chapter Nine

Bathsheba
Are Women As Powerless As They Appear?

When Bill Clinton won the presidential elections, he was elated. He and his wife Hillary decided to sneak off to celebrate. On their way, they stopped to put gasoline in their car. Bill could not help noticing the way Hillary was talking with the gas pump attendant.

As they drove off, Bill said to Hillary, "I could not help noticing the way you were talking with the attendant, like you were old friends."

"Of course," Hillary replied, "we knew each other a long time ago. We were in high school together. In fact, we dated for a while, and he even asked me to marry him."

Bill swelled with pride. "Aren't you glad you turned him down, and married the president of the United States instead?"

"If I had married him," Hillary replied, "he would have been the president and you, the gas pump attendant."[203]

How men underestimate women! As of Hillary, could it be also of Bathsheba? A commentator, male, described her as "a good-natured, rather stupid woman who was a natural prey both to more passionate and to cleverer men."[204] Is she as naïve and dumb as she appears to be? A closer look at her may help us see something more than meets the eye. She features prominently in King David's life, at the height of his power, and the ebb of his life. At his prime, his generals fought his battles while he loafed at home. As he loitered on the roof of his palace, Bathsheba caught his attention. The account of David's fall into adultery with her and the subsequent murder of her husband seem to portray her as a helpless victim.[205]

Was she really innocent? Even if we grant that her bathing nude in full view of the palace had no impure motives, questions could be raised about her actions later. Why did she confide with David about her pregnancy but say not a word to her husband, Uriah? Was it to protect him from the king, or to leverage on a secret between her and the king? Surely, she knew David's scheme when Uriah was ordered home from the battlefront. Did she make any attempt to sleep with Uriah so that he would think the child in her womb was his?

When Uriah returned drunk from David's drinking party, did Bathsheba make any attempt to get him into bed with her? She probably waited, and then assumed that he had slept at the servants' quarters as he did the night before when he was sober. The days passed with Bathsheba playing her part as accomplice—willing or unwilling— to the cover-up. When Plan A (to get Uriah to sleep with his wife) failed, and also Plan B (to get Uriah drunk so that he would sleep with his wife), she probably second-guessed the king's Plan C (to send Uriah back to the frontlines and have him killed in battle).

Perhaps, she was truly helpless to do anything, but we cannot be sure if she was truly innocent. To be summoned by the king to his palace, to be invited by an admirer to his bed, and to be impregnated with the seed of the royal line—could Bathsheba see this as an opportunity to be part of the royal family? If so, she had her wish fulfilled. Uriah met his end, she discharged the days of mourning and became David's wife.

Some three decades passed, and we meet Bathsheba again, an older woman but still a force to be reckoned with in David's old age. The king who once stood high on the palace roof with nothing to do, now lay low on his bed unable to do anything. Yet Bathsheba, together with the prophet Nathan, roused the king from his lethargy to proclaim her son Solomon successor and king. No small feat for a woman, especially when her son was not the eldest in line to the throne. Did Bathsheba acquire the skill to manipulate her way into the king's heart, or did she possess that skill from the start? She joined David's harem as the seventh wife, and yet made her way past the others to be David's favourite.[206]

KING-MAKER AND QUEEN MOTHER

Even Nathan who knew the dark secret of her life allied with her. The prophet no doubt saw her as more than a pawn—she was a queen and more, a king-maker. She gave Israel a most illustrious king under whom the kingdom grew and flourished like it never did before, or thereafter. Surely, the good we see in Solomon must reflect the good in his mother. According to Jewish tradition, Proverbs 31 was penned by Solomon in memory of his mother.

> "Though there is a question about whether the Book of Proverbs was written by her son, it bears a striking relationship to her life, opening as it does with many dark pictures of a woman as man's seductress, but closing happily with the picture of the ideal woman who is a trusted companion and devoted mother."[207]

Indeed the way the compiler brackets the book with references to women points to his mixed feelings about the fairer sex. He had seen the worst and the best in them. He chose to begin with a warning against the worst, and to end with a tribute to the best. It may be far-fetched to think that Bathsheba's life story inspired this framework, but the thought does have its appeal.

After Bathsheba succeeded in making her son king, she featured in one more episode in the succession process. Adonijah approached her to speak to Solomon about a request: "Please ask King Solomon—he will not refuse you—to give me Abishag the Shunammite as my wife."[208] Abishag was David's concubine before he died, and to ask for her was tantamount to asking for David's throne.[209] Knowing Adonijah, we are not surprised at such a foolish move—his attempt earlier on to crown himself king was foolhardy. But did Bathsheba see the implication of such a request? If she did, she made no attempt to dissuade Adonijah from it. We wonder if she simply saw this as an opportunity to seal the fate of someone who was only recently her son's arch-rival. One commentator portrays her thus:

> "....Who would understand harem politics more than the queen of the harem? ...She cooperates with Nathan, exposes Adonijah, and generally makes prudent moves in the halls of power. Thus, it is evident that she understands the nature of Adonijah's request and prudently warns her son of his rival's inept power play."[210]

On the other hand, it could be that she saw nothing in Adonijah's request other than a loser claiming a consolation prize. She passed on the request to Solomon who blew his top: "What kind of favor is this, asking that Abishag the Shunammite be given to Adonijah? Why don't you just ask me to hand over the whole kingdom to him on a platter since he is my older brother and has Abiathar the priest and Joab son of Zeruiah on his side!"[211] Solomon directed his outrage, first at his mother, accusing her of collusion with his detractors; then he turned on Adonijah, ordering his execution.

Thereafter, Bathsheba slipped out of the narrative, never to appear again. Did she fall from grace with her son and fade into oblivion? The narrator does not tell us—evidently, Bathsheba's role in Solomon's succession is concluded, and nothing more need to be said. But she did leave a mark on all future kings. They would always be mentioned with the names of their mothers. Even an individual like Jeroboam, not from the royal line but destined to become king, was introduced with his mother's name.

"So far two royal mothers have been named in I Kings, Solomon's and Adonijah's, both in the context of their sons' potential for becoming king. Later, as we shall see, whenever a king succeeds to the throne of David, his mother's name will be given. Naming Jeroboam's mother here is a subtle prefiguring of his royal destiny."[212]

This literary device stands as a tribute to Bathsheba and the pivotal role of a queen-mother—for better or for worse. If Bathsheba's role worked out for the better, that of another queen-mother worked out for the worse. We turn our attention to Athaliah, another influential female figure in the succession of kings. The daughter of Ahab, king of Israel, she married Jehoram, king of Judah, probably in a marriage of political expediency. Ahab and Jehoram's father, Jehoshaphat, had been good friends. Athaliah subsequently distinguished herself as the only queen to rule Judah. Like her mother Jezebel, she worshipped the god Baal, a foreign deity which both women imported from abroad and promoted in Israel and Judah.

POWERFUL WOMEN

Jehoram was killed in battle and their son Ahaziah reigned briefly with Athaliah as queen-mother. When he died prematurely from battle wounds, she seized power and proceeded to eliminate the entire royal family. What kind of a woman was she to murder her own grandchildren? Was it necessary since she could easily have continued as queen-mother? But her ambition to be queen and sole ruler blinded her to reason and robbed her of all human feelings. During the reign of her husband, she was probably the instigator behind the murder of his brothers. During the reign of her son, she was no doubt the influence behind his desecration of the temple and his promotion of Baal worship.[213]

Ironically, her lust for power would be thwarted by another woman: Jehosheba, the daughter of Jehoram and the wife of Jehoiada the priest. She rescued Ahaziah's youngest son, Joash, the sole survivor of the massacre, and hid him. Athaliah's reign lasted six years during which her apostasy wasted the nation and her brutality wearied the people. Her rule ended when the priest presented Joash as the rightful heir to the throne, and no one stood with her when she cried, "Treason! Treason!" Like her mother, she met an ignominious death. [214]

> "In her miserable end, Athaliah bore a resemblance to her mother Jezebel, who was abandoned to the dogs. Athaliah was left in a horse-path, to be trampled upon. Like her mother she died a queen, but without a hand to help her or an eye to pity her."[215]

Athaliah and Bathsheba represent a breed of women who wield power, overtly or covertly, over men. History would tell similar stories of such women.

Cleopatra ruled with her father Ptolemy XII in the last century before Christ. When he died, she married his brother who ruled as Ptolemy XIII, as required by the Egyptian custom. She did the same with another brother who ruled as Ptolemy XIV. But ruling as queen only whetted her appetite for the ultimate power base in Egypt—she eventually assumed the throne as sole Pharaoh. To consolidate her position, she forged a liaison with Julius Caesar, and later with Mark Antony. Her influence straddled the power blocs of her time, Egyptian and Roman. The way she charmed and conquered one man after another led the philosopher Blaise Pascal to muse, "Cleopatra's nose, had it been shorter, the whole face of the world would have been changed."[216]

Cixi Taihou, better known as the Empress Dowager, ruled the Manchu Qing Dynasty in China for almost 50 years before her death in 1908. Added to the harem while still an adolescent, she rose through the ranks to give the Emperor Xianfeng a son and successor. Upon

Xianfeng's death, she dismissed the regents appointed by him, took their place, and eventually assumed absolute rule over the empire, with her son (and later her nephew) reigning only in name. So tight was her grip on power that the Qing Dynasty could not continue without her; it disintegrated soon after her death.[217]

Do we not see resemblances in these women with Bathsheba and Athaliah? We may add women like Helen of Troy, part human and part goddess, over whom a war was fought and by whose face a thousand ships were launched. Then there is Josephine, the first wife of Napoleon Bonaparte, whom he divorced, presumably because she bore him no children. Despite numerous affairs, divorce and remarriage, the emperor's last words as he lay dying in exile on St. Helena were: "France, the Army, the Head of the Army, Josephine."[218] Such power that women wield over men continues to recent times—in legendary figures like Eva Peron of Argentina, Imelda Marcos of the Philippines and Princess Diana of Britain.

ANONYMOUS WOMEN

But women need not be prominent to exert influence. Biblical women such as Bathsheba and Athaliah are given considerable attention in Scriptures which ensures the memory of their names. In contrast are women who appear silently and disappear anonymously. In an instructive study of Jeroboam's wife, Robin G. Branch comments on her story and her role:

> "Anonymous women like the wife of Jeroboam in this story accomplish two narrative purposes. First, they direct attention to the named male characters with whom they interact. Second, their anonymity deflects attention from them as people and highlights their roles."[219]

When their son fell ill, Jeroboam instructed his wife to seek counsel from the prophet Ahijah. The same prophet had earlier told

Jeroboam he would become king of ten tribes of Israel, and, if he followed the ways of the LORD, his kingdom would prosper. Jeroboam chose instead to forsake the LORD and follow after pagan idols. With his son sick and the succession in jeopardy, he sent his wife to inquire of the prophet.

Throughout the narrative, Jeroboam's wife remains unnamed and unheard. She utters not a word, while the men speak: her husband speaks to her, telling her what to do; the prophet speaks to her, telling her what to say to her husband. She acts as a silent messenger, moving back and forth, in mute compliance to their instructions. The narrative makes no attempt to name her, or to tell readers what she thought or how she felt. In fact, in the story, she plays her role as a woman in disguise, hiding her identity.

But her anonymity belies her role: she carries the voice of God's prophet back to her husband, declaring the death of their son, the end of his dynasty, and indeed the eventual collapse of the entire kingdom. Though she says nothing in the narrative, what she says to Jeroboam means everything to the reader. We now know what God is going to do, and how the whole story will end. Could there be an underlying message as to the role of women in the Bible: wordless, yet bearing the Word of God; nameless, yet achieving God's purpose?

Though the opening story of Bill and Hillary Clinton may be fictitious, it encapsulates the truth about the role of women in the lives of men. Consider, for example, the number of men who dedicate their books, Ph. D. theses and other such works to their wives, declaring that they could never had done it without their other halves. Women deserve such accolades but they must guard against the desire for vicarious power through their men. The mother of John and James came to Jesus, asking for them to be seated at the right and the left hand of Jesus when he established his kingdom.[220] She reminds us of queen-mothers like Bathsheba and the Empress Dowager who sought to put their sons on the throne.

POWER STRUGGLE AND SUBTLE INFLUENCE

Sometimes, women choose to go the whole way—like Athaliah and Cleopatra—and covet power for themselves. Such was the case of Miriam, the older sister of Moses. In an extreme case of sibling rivalry, she challenged Moses' authority, and demanded her share of it: "Has the LORD indeed spoken only through Moses? Has he not spoken through us also?"[221] Though she approached Moses with their brother Aaron, Miriam spoke for herself. But her questions sounded hollow for they came in the wake of the appointment of 70 elders to share in Moses' burden of leadership.

Perhaps, Miriam still saw Moses as her baby brother whom she helped save from death a long time ago. She resented his marriage to a foreigner, a Cushite woman, and used that as an excuse to dispute Moses' supremacy. The outcome of the challenge showed Miriam had fallen foul of God who struck her with leprosy and banished her from the camp for a week. The episode reminds us that women can be as hungry for power as men. Miriam had already played her role as a prophetess with the women looking up to her.[222] But that was not enough, and she wanted more.

Of course, women are not the only ones who over-reach for power. Men do too. In the final analysis, men and women stand equally capable of the right use of power and equally culpable for its wrong use. The difference may be that men wield power more visibly than women who exert their influence more subtly. On two occasions when I stepped down from my position and handed it to a successor, my wife played a significant role. In the first, she observed that I was going to bed early and asked if my work had lost its challenge. I used to work late past midnight, but with two competent associate pastors my workload had lightened. Within a year after her comment, I submitted my resignation, and one of my associate pastors took over. He has since served more than the 17 years I served—which would qualify for a successful succession.

In the second instance, my wife observed that I was having difficulty working with my senior colleague as well as meeting my revised job description—which required more an administrator than a pastor-teacher. "Your days are numbered," she remarked. In a frank discussion with my colleague, he graciously released me from my position. I gave a twelve-month notice at the end of which the organisation found someone to take my place. Those were the only two occasions in my thirty-year ministry when I stepped down from a position. In each case, it came as a result of my wife's perceptive observation and intuitive grasp of the situation.

Women feature more significantly in succession stories than we choose to remember or care to admit. A man's rise to power or a fall from it may result from the words of a woman. Perhaps a Spanish proverb says it best: "A woman's advice is of little value, but he who does not take it is a fool." The words of Bathsheba to the dying King David provide ample proof of such a paradox.

BATHSHEBA
For Reflection and Discussion

1.   In the account of David's adultery with Bathsheba, how much was she a victim and how much was she an accomplice? Do you think she was helpless in the whole affair?

2.   After Bathsheba, every king's mother was named together with the king. How is this a tribute to the role Bathsheba played as queen mother? Consider the parts she played in Solomon's ascension to the throne and in Adonijah's execution.

3.   How was Athaliah similar to Bathsheba or different from her? How does Athaliah foreshadow powerful women like Cleopatra and the Empress Dowager? Give an example in recent times, and discuss the role such women play in the making and unmaking of world leaders.

4.   Why were certain women not named (e.g. Jeroboam's wife) though they played important roles? What do these anonymous women tell us about how God works in history?

5.   Discuss the proverb: "A woman's advice is of little value, but he who does not take it is a fool." Give personal examples, if any, of the truth or untruth of this paradox.

Chapter Ten

Peter
Why Should We Talk About Death?

On a foggy day in the spring of 2010, an air crash near Smolensk in western Russia killed the Polish President Lech Kaczynski, and wiped out Poland's ruling elite. The chief of the armed forces, the head of the navy, the central bank governor, opposition lawmakers and Kaczynski's wife Maria were among those who perished in the crash. Thankfully, analysts concurred with Goldman Sachs' assessment, "Although tragic, we do not believe that this event threatens the political and financial stability in Poland in any fundamental way." [223]

No one can hear such headline news without feeling sorrow for the people affected. Yet, beyond the shock and grief, there lies a lesson which we all must grasp. I am reminded of an exercise that put to test a board meeting of executive staff. Someone walked into the room and read an announcement with a deadpan face: "Gentlemen, we have just received news that an American Airlines plane had crashed off the coast of Florida. I am sorry to inform you that our President and Vice-President were on board. There were no survivors."

After a few moments of silence, the staff began their deliberation. "Who is next in line after the President and Vice-President?" "Who will take charge and make an official announcement?" "Do we have a policy about the Vice-President travelling in the same plane with the President?" And so the discussion continued. Though it was only an exercise, the men in the room knew the seriousness of such a situation if it ever occurred. How many boards or councils would consider such an exercise? How many senior pastors, CEOs, or founder-presidents would give such a scenario serious thought?

The leader of a small band of disciples certainly did. Jesus spoke often about his departure, and prepared his followers for it. In the Gospel of Mark, the "hinge" between the two halves turns on a sombre announcement by Jesus of his death. All that Jesus did and taught leads up to it, and thereafter all that he did and taught flows from it. At the mid-point of the account of Jesus' life, Mark the gospel-writer places two significant events: the confession of Peter at Caesarea Philippi, and the transfiguration of Jesus soon after. Each is followed by Jesus' talk of death.[224]

At Caesarea Philippi, Jesus had conducted an opinion poll, asking the disciples who people thought he was. When they had given their feedback, he asked them who they thought he was. As usual, Peter was the first to speak, "You are the Christ, the Son of the living God." Presumably, he spoke on behalf of the disciples; however, the blessing pronounced by Jesus was conferred primarily on him:

> "Blessed are you, Simon Bar-Jonah! For flesh and blood has not revealed this to you, but my Father who is in heaven. And I tell you, you are Peter, and on this rock I will build my church, and the gates of hell shall not prevail against it. I will give you the keys of the kingdom of heaven, and whatever you bind on earth shall be bound in heaven, and whatever you loose on earth shall be loosed in heaven."[225]

From one perspective, Jesus was declaring his successor. Calling him by his full name, Simon Bar-Jonah, Jesus repeated another name he had given him earlier: *Cephas* in Aramaic or *Peter* in Greek, meaning *Rock*.[226] The aura of formality around these words makes *Peter* sound more like a title. Perhaps, it was meant to be so. The honour and authority Jesus accorded him—or his title—was considerable. Upon him Jesus would build his church, and to him Jesus would give the keys of the kingdom.

BIG NOISE AND SMALL VOICE

Interpreters have debated if "Peter" and "this rock" refer to the same thing. The Catholic tradition claims that Peter is indeed the rock, and from that claim, makes him the first bishop of Rome, starting a line of apostolic succession which leads to the present Pope. To avoid that, the Protestant tradition differentiates Peter from the rock, noting that *Peter* is masculine while *rock* is feminine; hence the church is built upon Peter's confession of Christ rather than on Peter himself. Michael Green points out the merits in each view:

> "...if the Catholics are right in thinking it is primarily Peter, albeit the believing Peter, who becomes the church's rock-man, the Protestants are surely right in pointing out that the passage contains no hints that this role should devolve on any successors in Rome or anywhere else."[227]

The natural reading of the text makes Peter the rock, but nowhere makes him an absolute or infallible ruler. When Jesus began talking about his death, Peter took him aside and rebuked him: "Far be it from you, Lord! This shall never happen to you!" One moment Jesus saw in Peter's confession the revelation of his Father, the next he saw in Peter's protest the instigation of Satan: "Get behind me, Satan! You are a hindrance to me."[228] The successor to Jesus, the founder of the church, and the keeper of her gates, was after all human, like any of the other disciples.

As it turned out, Peter faltered on several occasions, his faults all the more glaring because of his impetuous nature and his leadership position. Caught off-guard in situations when he did not know what to say, Peter spoke anyway. Typical of leaders who make waves by making noise, Peter opened his mouth and put his foot in it. Howard

Behar, former president of Starbucks International, shares from the coffee industry some leadership principles he has learned. He quotes a typically cryptic Chinese saying, "Big noise on stairs, nobody coming down." To Behar, *Starbucks* represents:

> "… a place to get a cup of coffee your way; a place for friendly, romantic, business or political conversation; a place to work, think, read, or simply be with yourself. Ultimately, Starbucks is and was a place where people can come and sit and reflect on a rainy Saturday afternoon. A place for our customers to listen for their still, small voice. Not the Big Noise."[229]

It took Peter a while to stop making noise long enough to hear himself and his Lord. At the transfiguration, he uttered, "Rabbi, it is good that we are here. Let us make three tents, one for you and one for Moses and one for Elijah." But a voice from heaven silenced him: "This is my beloved Son—listen to him!"[230] Peter would fumble a few more times, notably when he declared that even if all the other disciples forsook Jesus, he would never do such a thing: "Even if I must die with you, I will not deny you!" He ended up denying the Lord thrice.[231] Jesus knew Peter's faults, and foreknew his failures—yet, he declared Peter his successor.

We are left in no doubt that, in the eyes of Jesus, Peter occupied a special place among the twelve chosen disciples. His name is always listed first, and together with James and John forms the inner circle of Jesus. He speaks on behalf of the disciples, and Jesus addresses him when he speaks to the disciples.[232] Despite his failure to live up to his boast of loyalty, Jesus continues to single him out for attention. He is probably the first man to see Jesus after the resurrection, and the only disciple to be named in Jesus' instruction to meet in Galilee.[233] There by the Sea of Galilee, Jesus re-enacts two scenes: one, when Peter gave up fishing to follow Jesus, and another, when Peter lost his nerve and denied following Jesus. He takes Peter a full circle, helps him close the loop on his failure, and commissions him afresh.[234]

NEITHER SHADOW NOR SPONGE

After Jesus ascended to heaven, Peter continued as the established leader. He initiated the filling of the vacancy left by Judas, acted as spokesman for the disciples on the day of Pentecost, and as spokesman to the authorities when opposition arose. Peter administered discipline against Ananias and Sapphira, endorsed the work among the Samaritans, and took the lead in the mission to the Gentiles. In these acts, Peter played the role of a midwife in the birth of the church. He exercised the prerogative and the "keys" given to him by Jesus. With those keys, he opened the doors of the kingdom to Jews, Samaritans and Gentiles. With the same keys, he closed the doors to those who opposed God, openly or subtly.

We last hear of Peter when he stood up at the Jerusalem Council and spoke on the side of the Gentile converts. Thereafter he drops out of the narrative, having fulfilled his role as a successor of his master. How could such an unpromising candidate for succession turn out the way he did? When Jesus called him "a rock," he was anything but one. Indeed, Jesus once described him as "chaff," lightweight and liable to be scattered to the winds. Yet, Jesus consistently affirmed him, and patiently groomed him to become the chief of the apostles.

No one could have followed Jesus, listened to his teaching, and witnessed his miracles without feeling overwhelmed and intimidated— much less Peter and the band of disciples. They shrank back in awe when he calmed the storm, clammed up in embarrassment when he caught them arguing about status, and answered Jesus with blank looks when he quizzed them about the feeding of the multitudes.[235] Yet Jesus never belittled the disciples for their lack of power or understanding, however all-powerful and all-knowing he appeared to them. He always gave them space to err and to learn.

MaryKate Morse explores the issue of "social space" taken up by leaders. Their power varies from one end of the spectrum to the other, from those who are like shadows exercising no power to those who are like sponges absorbing all power.

> "Jesus never acted small. He wasn't a shadow who stayed in the background. On the other hand, Jesus never acted big, like a sponge soaking up lots of social space. Instead, he embedded his presence and power in his followers so that they might thrive."[236]

This is seen in the way Jesus encouraged initiative and invited involvement in his miracles. At the wedding feast when the wine ran out, he told the servants to fill the jars with water before he turned it into wine. At the feeding of the five thousand, he told the disciples to feed the people. When they came with a little boy's lunch, he multiplied it, and had the disciples distribute the food and collect the leftovers. At the raising of Lazarus, he asked the bystanders to remove the stone from the tomb before he raised Lazarus from the dead. After that, he asked them to remove the grave-clothes from Lazarus.

Jesus did only what others could not do: turning the water into wine, multiplying the loaves and fishes, raising the dead. In everything else, he involved the people around him. In that sense, he stood apart from leaders like Moses and Elijah who felt they must do everything, and consequently lapsed into self-pity and despair. Jesus also stood apart from kings like Solomon and Hezekiah who did nothing to ensure succession. As a result, they left behind sons, Rehoboam and Manasseh, who undid all the good they had done.

Jesus knew his time was short. He began his ministry, working in a limited area, teaching on his own. Soon he called to himself twelve men who would travel with him, as they moved in an ever-widening circle. They would watch him, listen to him, and learn from him. In time, crowds would throng to Jesus. They came by the hundreds and thousands, giving him neither space to move nor time to rest. Yet, Jesus harboured no illusion about his popularity. He never allowed the crowds to determine his agenda, but retreated to take instructions from his Father.[237]

THE FEW AMONG THE MANY

Jesus stayed focused on his mission, one eye towards Jerusalem where he would fulfil his destiny, and the other on the Twelve who would take over after him. While he continued to minister to all who came to him, Jesus spent much of his time with his twelve chosen men. They would be witnesses of his life, and would later bear witness to the same.

> "In the training of the twelve for the work of the apostleship, hearing and seeing the words and works of Christ necessarily occupied an important place. Eye and ear witnessing of the facts of an unparalleled life was an indispensable preparation for future witness-bearing. The apostles could secure credence for their wondrous tale only by being able to preface it with the protestation: 'That which we have seen and heard declare we unto you.'"[238]

As Jesus chose twelve out of the multitude, he chose three out of the twelve to be in his inner circle: Peter, John and James. On occasions, he allowed only the three to be with him: when he raised to life the daughter of Jairus at his home, when he revealed his glory at his transfiguration, and when he agonised in prayer in the Garden of Gethsemane.[239] The differentiation must have irked the other disciples, and led to their clamouring for similar positions.[240] Jesus intervened in their bickering to teach them about servant-leadership—but he continued to favour the three.

Many leaders serve the many and fail to pay attention to the few. Jesus ministered to huge crowds but gave time to the twelve and the three. Though they heard him when he spoke to the crowds, he took them aside to process with them what they heard and saw. He explained the meaning of the parables he told; in private he answered their questions about the destruction of the temple. He placed them in situations where they would be tested, then came to their rescue when they could not handle the crises. Once he slept while the disciples battled a storm against their boat. Another time, he sent them across the lake, and came walking on water to them when they struggled to keep afloat.[241]

The greatest test Jesus put his disciples through was when he allowed himself to be arrested, and the disciples to be scattered. He had forewarned them: "You will all fall away because of me this night. For it is written, 'I will strike the shepherd, and the sheep of the flock will be scattered.'"[242] Jesus likened his followers to sheep, and himself the shepherd. In another place, he called himself the "good shepherd" who knew his sheep, who called each of them by name, and who would give his life for them.[243] This analogy has become the standard portrayal of the leader and followers in Christian circles, often with the focus shifting from the good shepherd to the obedient sheep.

At a church board meeting, the pastor announced his decision on a matter under discussion, and asked, Amen? The board members responded, Baa! Perhaps, that did not really happen, but we would not be surprised if it did. Many followers, like these board members, feel they have no choice but to follow blindly their leader. John Edmund Haggai relates an experience he had visiting the Middle East, the land of his forefathers. When he arrived in Lebanon, he found a thriving Christian community that had been founded by Western missionaries. Seeing in Haggai a compatriot, the local believers bared their souls to him:

> "John, we love the missionaries, but they treat us like children. We are not satisfied to be marionettes on the end of a Western string. That offends us. The work of God suffers because we are not treated as equals. The missionaries love us; they're willing to die for us, but they are not willing to share their ministry."[244]

This is evidently not the case with Jesus. Granted, the disciples behaved at times like children, and he chided them as such—but he nurtured them into mature adults. He spoke of them as sheep, but he raised them to become shepherds. Those of us in public service face a dilemma when people are entrusted to our charge. How can we serve them without becoming paternalistic on the one hand, and mercenary on the other? Such a tension troubled me when I was engaged as an interim pastor to help a church resolve some leadership issues. A couple asked me about my role and surprised me with their candour, "So you are coming to our church as a consultant. You are going to tell us what is wrong with us, let us solve our problems, wash your hands and then leave us."

ABANDONING THE FLOCK IN DEATH

Another person reminded me of what Jesus said in John 10, and urged me, "Please be our shepherd, not a hireling." A hireling, according to Jesus, would flee when a wolf appears because the sheep do not belong to him. In contrast, the shepherd who owns the sheep would stay and risk his life for his sheep.[245] Yet we need to be careful not to press the analogy too far. Founders of churches, organisations and businesses lead with an ardent sense of ownership. They view their work as part of their "family," and consequently find it hard to cede control of their "family jewels." They end up claiming ultimate authority and demanding unquestioning compliance of their followers.[246] Strictly speaking, the shepherd and sheep analogy applies only to Jesus. Only Jesus the Chief Shepherd owns the sheep. We, like Peter, serve as under-shepherds, accountable to the owner and master.[247]

When the air crash in Russia decimated the Polish elite, the country had those who are next in line to take over. What if there were none? For several years, I was a guest speaker of a church founded by a Chinese businessman. His generosity knew no bounds. He invited my wife to fly with me, hosted us in the best hotels and finest restaurants. He had pioneered the church a decade earlier, and funded most of its operations. A staff of pastors led the services held in a shopping mall, while plans for the purchase of land for a new building were being finalised.

Then I heard news that the founder suffered a massive heart attack and died. Soon afterwards, I preached at the church which was still reeling in a state of shock. But a greater shock awaited me: none of the leaders knew what to do, for none of them had ever been part of any policy-making or decision-making body. The founder had all along managed a one-man operation. Like many in the church, I felt utterly helpless.

As under-shepherds, we owe it to the flock and to the Chief Shepherd, to recognise our mortality and to prepare our people for our departure. As someone once put it, speaking of the long-serving pastor of his church, "We know he will die *for* us, but we are worried he may die *on* us." To leave our sheep without someone to take care of them would make us no different from the hireling—one abandons the sheep in life, and the other, in death.

PETER
For Reflection and Discussion

1.   Why are people reluctant to talk about death? Why do leaders shy from talking about their exit from life and how it affects their exit from their position?

2.   Why did Jesus keep reminding his disciples of his death? How did he prepare them for it?

3.   Jesus announced his successor in Peter. Was Peter ready for such a position? How did Jesus nurture the Twelve and in particular Peter to assume responsibility after him?

4.   On the shepherd and sheep analogy, what is the difference between a hireling and the shepherd? How can ownership of the sheep be taken to an extreme, especially when the emphasis shifts from the good shepherd to the obedient sheep? Who really owns the sheep?

5.   How do we prepare our loved ones and followers for our departure? How can we overcome cultural norms and personal discomfort to discuss something that is certain as death?

Chapter Eleven

Barnabas
Can One Set the Course Without Steering the Ship?

On 13 June 1964, Nelson Mandela arrived on Robben Island to serve his sentence. Convicted for his struggle against apartheid rule in South Africa, he would spend his life in a small cell on an island cut off from the world. On 11 February 1990, at the age of 72, he walked out a free man. He had spent 25 years and eight months in prison. With apartheid dismantled, Mandela became the hero of the people, and within a few years, the president of the nation. He could have stayed on as president for life. But a year into his office, in 1995, he declared he would step down at the end of the first term, saying that "an octogenarian shouldn't be meddling in politics."[248]

Like him, other political prisoners in Africa had become presidents, among them Kenyatta in Kenya, Nkrumah in Ghana, and Mugabe in Zimbabwe. Mandela distinguished himself as one who left office voluntarily. He turned down a second five-year term, content, in the words of Cyril Ramaphosa, "to set the course, not steer the ship."[249] As Richard Stengel rightly sums it up, "…Mandela's greatest act of leadership was the renunciation of it."[250]

Stepping aside for another is a rare quality in leadership. Only exceptional leaders know how to do it, voluntarily, judiciously and graciously. Barnabas excelled as one of such rare leaders. In his ministry and travels with Paul, his name always came first—understandably so, for Barnabas became a Christian before Paul, served in the church before Paul, and encouraged the people while Paul was terrorising them. Yet, in time, the order was reversed to "Paul and Barnabas" and became consistently so in the Acts narrative.[251] Such a change speaks volumes, especially in cultures that value protocol. Barnabas had relinquished his leadership to another.

Not only did he step down, he soon stepped out of the narrative altogether. In Luke's account of the early years of the church, two great apostles took up the larger parts of his 28 chapters. The lives and exploits of Peter and of Paul leave the reader in no doubt that they led the fledgling church and steered the ship. In between the two apostles, Luke inserted one other person who brought the apostles together: Barnabas. Without him and the part he played, the second half of Acts could have been different. If great men like Peter and Paul were likened to flaming torches, Barnabas would be the small match that lit them.

Luke mentions Barnabas 23 times, beginning at the fourth chapter. After describing the momentous birth of the church and the subsequent opposition against it, Luke takes a pause and profiles two contrasting individuals in the infant church. He first introduces Barnabas, and then contrasts him with Ananias and his wife Sapphira. While the couple craved public honour and faked their generosity to gain it, Barnabas had recognition conferred on him by the apostles. Joseph (his original name) was given the name, *Barnabas,* meaning *a son of encouragement*[252]—an idea that could have come from Peter whose name was given him by Jesus.

By birth, Barnabas was a Levite, from the tribe that provided the Temple with its assistants to the priests. His family migrated to Cyprus where Barnabas was born into the sizeable Jewish population there. Barnabas chose to return and make his residence in Jerusalem where he owned property, indicating that the ancient law forbidding

Levites to own land no longer applied. Born and raised as a Jew of the Diaspora, Barnabas would be comfortable with Greek-speaking Jews, also known as the Hellenists—a fact that would become significant later.

In the Jerusalem church, Barnabas distinguished himself an encourager to the people. His act of generosity, in selling a piece of property and giving its proceeds to the church for the needy, made an impression on Peter and the apostles. The name they gave him, *Barnabas*, stuck with him as he went on to live out its meaning. His encouragement would make a lasting difference in the lives of two individuals and a church, with repercussions stretching far beyond Jerusalem.

THUNDERBOLT TO LIGHTNING ROD

The first individual to profit from Barnabas' encouragement was Saul the persecutor before he became Paul the apostle. After his life-changing Damascus Road experience, Saul found himself caught between his erstwhile allies and his former foes. The Jews in Damascus sought to kill him for betraying the faith, while the Christians in Jerusalem shunned him on suspicion that his conversion was a ploy. Only Barnabas believed Saul.

> "And when he [Saul] had come to Jerusalem, he attempted to join the disciples. And they were all afraid of him, for they did not believe that he was a disciple. But Barnabas took him and brought him to the apostles and declared to them how on the road he had seen the Lord, who spoke to him, and how at Damascus he had preached boldly in the name of Jesus. So he went in and out among them at Jerusalem, preaching boldly in the name of the Lord."[253]

From Paul's own account, this visit to Jerusalem took place three years after this conversion following which he withdrew to Arabia.

We know nothing of this period of his life, but may safely assume that he needed time to think through where his theology had gone wrong. He would later declare that the gospel he preached did not come from man, but "through a revelation of Jesus Christ"[254]—a reference to his time in Damascus and Arabia. With this lapse of three years, the suspicion of the Jerusalem believers becomes even more remarkable. The passage of time had not erased the dread they felt for Saul.

A recent film version of Paul's life shows him led by Barnabas under the cover of night to a secret rendezvous where they are met by James who sneers at Paul in disbelief as Peter waits hesitantly in the shadows.[255] We cannot be certain if that was the way it happened, but there must have been an element of doubt and distrust. Through the advocacy of Barnabas, Paul met the apostles and began preaching in Jerusalem. F. F. Bruce posits a probable scenario:

> "It appears... that Saul took up the work which Stephen had laid down at his death, by engaging in disputations with the Hellenists. Their reaction was swift and violent. Saul was worse than Stephen: he was in their eyes a traitor to the true cause, and by his volte-face he had let down those who formerly followed him loyally as their leader in suppressing the Christian movement."[256]

Not only was there a threat to his life, the threat extended to the believers in Jerusalem as well. The thunderbolt against the church had become a lightning rod against the church. The believers, fearing for his life, took him to the Mediterranean seaport of Caesarea and shipped him off to his native home in Tarsus. Luke adds a telling note following this send-off: "So the church throughout all Judea and Galilee and Samaria had peace and was being built up. And walking in the fear of the Lord and in the comfort of the Holy Spirit, it multiplied."[257]

We can picture the people heaving a shared sigh of relief on seeing Paul depart and peace return to the region. They probably thought they had seen the last of Paul, but not so for Barnabas. He had believed Saul when he spoke about his conversion (and no doubt his call to preach the gospel to the Gentiles), and continued to believe Paul though his ministry in Jerusalem was cut short.

DAUGHTER CHURCH DIFFERENT FROM MOTHER

Preaching the gospel to the Gentiles must be a thought that stirred Barnabas' imagination. Like Paul, he grew up in the Diaspora where Jews and Gentiles mingled in cosmopolitan cities. Not long afterwards, word came to the leadership in Jerusalem that a daughter church in Antioch of Syria had embarked on something never done before.

"Now those who were scattered because of the persecution that arose over Stephen traveled as far as Phoenicia and Cyprus and Antioch, speaking the word to no one except Jews. But there were some of them, men of Cyprus and Cyrene, who on coming to Antioch spoke to the Hellenists also, preaching the Lord Jesus. And the hand of the Lord was with them, and a great number who believed turned to the Lord."[258]

Antioch was the third largest city in the Empire, after Rome and Alexandria, and hosted a large Jewish community. A missiologist compares the situation then to what happened in Los Angeles in the 1980s and 1990s when Korean missionaries came to the city and preached the gospel to the Korean migrants residing in what was called Koreatown. They met with such success that among the first-generation Korean-Americans, nearly 70% professed to be Christians.[259] Likewise, the Jews from Jerusalem went and preached the gospel to Jews in Antioch. As those from South Korea ministered within their own community, so those from Jerusalem ministered within their own synagogues.

But the Jews from Cyprus and Cyrene did something different—they took the gospel to the Gentiles.[260] Unlike those who came from Jerusalem, these Jews of the Diaspora carried no baggage tied to their ethnicity. Perhaps, it was Antioch itself that made the difference.

"The atmosphere of Antioch was as different as could be from that of Jerusalem. In this busy northern capital, a commercial city where European and Asiatic met, where Greek civilisation touched the Syrian desert, men naturally got their rough corners rubbed off, and religious differences that loomed so large in Judea began to look far less important."[261]

No wonder, what happened in Antioch raised concern with the mother church in Jerusalem which decided to despatch Barnabas to investigate and assess the radical turn of events.[262] By this time, Barnabas had gained recognition as a pillar of the church, and was chosen for that reason, and possibly because he would connect well with the men from Cyprus his home country. Luke tells us that Barnabas saw the work among the Gentles and affirmed it, and was himself affirmed with qualities that marked him as a *good man*.

"When he came and saw the grace of God, he was glad, and he exhorted them all to remain faithful to the Lord with steadfast purpose, for he was a good man, full of the Holy Spirit and of faith. And a great many people were added to the Lord."[263]

It takes someone like Barnabas to see beneath the surface to the grace of God. He had seen beneath the persecutor Saul to the grace of God working in his life. He saw in Antioch the same grace bringing Jews and Gentiles together into the church. Neither previous reputation nor prevailing convention prejudiced him against what God was doing, so full was Barnabas of the Spirit's fruit of love and God's gift of faith. He lived out his name as *a son of encouragement* and urged the church in Antioch to press on.

As the work continued to grow, Barnabas thought of Paul, and went to Tarsus in search of him. We can imagine the conversation between them when they met:

> Barnabas: "Come, and work with me."
> Paul: "The believers in Jerusalem don't trust me. I don't think they have forgiven me for what I did."
> Barnabas: "No, I'm not asking you to go to Jerusalem. We are going to Antioch."
> Paul: "Will the people there accept me?"
> Barnabas: "Don't worry—they are different. We are a church reaching out to the Gentiles."
> Paul: "You mean the pagans?"
> Barnabas: "Yes, don't you remember your call to bring the gospel to the Gentiles?"

Perhaps that was how Barnabas convinced Paul to leave Tarsus and return to Syria where memories of the Damascus Road and its aftermath still ran deep. As he had believed in Paul's conversion, so he believed in Paul's calling. The church in Antioch would provide a perfect setting and a fresh start for Paul to fulfill his commission to bear the name of Jesus to the Gentiles. So it did: for a whole year, the partnership of the two saw many more disciples added to the church.

FORGING A TEAM, FINDING A PLACE

Barnabas and Paul bonded and became an outstanding team, not only in Antioch but also in Jerusalem. On two occasions, they represented the daughter church to her mother church. Once, when a famine hit Jerusalem, they brought an offering. Another time, when a controversy arose over whether Gentiles should be circumcised, they argued their case against it. In between these visits, Barnabas was sent by the church, together with Paul, assisted by John Mark, on their first missionary journey.

Their expedition began with Cyprus as the first stop. Familiar ground for Barnabas, being his birth country, he naturally assumed leadership. But the next stop saw two changes to the team: Paul took over as leader, and Mark left for home.[264] We are unsure if the changes are related—did Mark leave because Barnabas was no longer in charge? More likely, the demands of travel, and perhaps, homesickness, prompted his departure at Perga. From that coastal city, a rough trail led up into the mountains, a formidable challenge for any novice. Paul and Barnabas braved the arduous journey, preaching the gospel first to the Jews of the Diaspora. A defining moment came for Paul after he spoke in a synagogue on the Sabbath day in Antioch of Pisidia.

> "The next Sabbath almost the whole city gathered to hear the word of the Lord. But when the Jews saw the crowds, they were filled with jealousy and began to contradict what was spoken by Paul, reviling him. And Paul and Barnabas spoke out boldly, saying, 'It was necessary that the word of God be spoken first to you. Since you thrust it aside and judge yourselves unworthy of eternal life, behold, we are turning to the Gentiles.'"[265]

Paul at last found his mission: he had fulfilled his obligation to his fellow-Jews; his conscience absolved him and cleared the way for him to go to the Gentiles. Nevertheless, the opposition from the Jews followed Paul. They pursued him to Lystra where he was stoned and left for dead. Luke tells us that the converts in Lystra took care of Paul and nursed him back to health. Could Barnabas be the one who rallied their help? If so, Paul owed Barnabas another debt. They made it to their next city, Derbe, their last, and then began their return journey, revisiting the converts and appointing elders to lead the new churches.

> "When they had preached the gospel to that city [Derbe] and had made many disciples, they returned to Lystra and to Iconium and to Antioch, strengthening the souls of the disciples, encouraging them to continue in the faith, and

saying that through many tribulations we must enter the kingdom of God. And when they had appointed elders for them in every church, with prayer and fasting they committed them to the Lord in whom they had believed."[266]

The missionary team had replicated what happened back home in Syrian Antioch: where a daughter church was planted by men from Cyprus and Cyrene, grand-daughter churches had sprouted across the sea in Asia Minor. Of note is the appointment of local leaders to take care of these churches.[267] Also of note is the precedence of Barnabas over Paul once they returned home. The reversed order of names, *Barnabas and Paul*, reflects Barnabas' standing—Paul might be the spokesman out in the mission field but back in Antioch, Barnabas held his ground as the acknowledged leader. His name comes first whenever the two of them are mentioned in relation to Antioch or Jerusalem.

Barnabas and Paul soon found themselves in Jerusalem where a council had been convened. The Jews who witnessed the conversion of the Gentiles had insisted that they be circumcised. In other words, these converts should become Jews as well when they became Christians. The Jerusalem Council decided against such a requirement, in favour of the delegation from Antioch, after hearing reports of "what signs and wonders God had done through them among the Gentiles."[268] The summary statements of two leading Jerusalem apostles, Peter and James, bracketed the reports of Barnabas and Paul which all heard in hushed silence.[269]

RECKLESSLY SPENDTHRIFT

With the decision of the Council, the loop was closed on Barnabas' mission in Antioch. He had been sent there from Jerusalem to assess the work. He had affirmed it, developed it and extended it. He had brought into it a most unlikely candidate, Saul, and paved the way for him to become Paul, the champion of the Gentiles. Barnabas was truly a pillar of strength to the church in Antioch, and a mainstay of encouragement to Paul. But the friendship of the two men, forged through the years of working together, would soon be tested.

When Paul proposed a second missionary journey to revisit the cities, churches and converts, Barnabas suggested taking Mark with them. When Paul objected, Barnabas insisted. The contention between them became so sharp that they went their separate ways: Paul took Silas, and Barnabas stuck with Mark. To Paul, Mark was a deserter who abandoned them and could not be trusted to go the distance. To Barnabas, Mark was a beginner who failed the first time and should be given a second chance. Why did Barnabas insist on taking Mark when he knew it would cost him his friendship with Paul? Probably for the same reason he stood with Saul the persecutor when he knew it would cost him his standing with the other disciples. As he saw in Saul something which others could not see, he saw in Mark what Paul could not see.

It is an irony that Paul who was given a second chance refused to give Mark the same. But years later, Barnabas would be proved right. In prison with only his personal physician with him, Paul thought of Mark: "Luke alone is with me. Get Mark and bring him with you, for he is very useful to me for ministry."[270] Prior to that, Mark was with Paul in Rome from where the apostle wrote his epistles to the Colossians and to Philemon, mentioning Mark's name.[271] It is believed that Mark also served as Peter's interpreter, and from him, heard witness accounts of Jesus' life and ministry. Mark went on to write the gospel, believed to be the first of the four written. Without Barnabas' encouragement, would we have Mark or Mark's Gospel?

Timothy Keller takes what is commonly known as the parable of the prodigal son, and turns the adjective on its head to describe also the father.

"The word 'prodigal' does not mean 'wayward' but, according to *Merriam-Webster's Collegiate Dictionary*, 'recklessly spendthrift.' It means to spend until you have nothing left. The term is therefore as appropriate for describing the father in the story as his younger son. The father's welcome to the repentant son was literally reckless, because he refused to 'reckon' or count his sin against him or demand repayment."[272]

The generosity of Barnabas may be understood in similar terms. His gift to the Jerusalem church from the sale of his property was but a token of his subsequent *prodigal* endowment of grace upon the Antioch church, upon Paul and upon Mark. He gave till he had nothing left to give, and silently disappeared from the pages of history. He had set the course for others to steer the ship.

BARNABAS
For Reflection and Discussion

1.   How does a leader set the course without steering the ship? Discuss how African leaders exemplify such leadership or else disavow it.

2.   How was Barnabas different from others in the way he received Saul the persecutor? While the other believers sent Saul home, what made Barnabas seek him out and bring him back?

3.   How was Barnabas "a son of encouragement" to the church at Antioch? In what ways was the daughter church different from the mother church in Jerusalem? How did Barnabas argue the case for the non-Jews at the Jerusalem Council?

4.   What led to the split between Paul and Barnabas? Imagine you are Mark—knowing you are the cause of it, describe how you feel towards Paul and towards Barnabas.

5.   Timothy Keller uses the adjective describing the "prodigal" son on the father who portrays God the Father. In what way is God "recklessly spendthrift" and how does it also describe Barnabas?

Chapter Twelve

Paul
How Do We Answer the Ultimate Question of Ownership?

In the final climactic scene of the epic *Star Wars*, Luke Skywalker refuses to join his father Darth Vader on the dark side of the Force. Emperor Palpatine takes over and unleashes his wrath on the helpless Luke. Darth Vader watches, torn between the pleas of his son and his loyalty to his master. His eyes shift back and forth from one to the other. His mind concentrates on a single question: *Am I Luke's father or am I the Emperor's servant?* He finally decides: he lifts the Emperor off his feet and casts him into the abyss. Darth Vader has answered the ultimate question of leadership.

The study of leadership has taken us down a long road. We once confronted the question, "*What* is leadership?" Definitions abounded as to whether it was vision, or influence, or some irreducible minimum without which leadership would not be leadership. Then came the question, "*Who* is a leader?" The focus shifted to the person rather than what he has or does. This turn in the road takes us in the right direction as we give attention to character, not just competence.

But the path to true leadership does not end there. We need to ask one more question, that of *Whose?* While the first two questions address the issues of competence and character, this third question forces the leader to come face to face with something even more fundamental, the issues of identity and ownership: *Whose* is the leader?[273] Paul of Tarsus, caught in a storm and about to be shipwrecked, called out above the cries of despair of those around him,

> "...I urge you to keep up your courage, because not one of you will be lost; only the ship will be destroyed. Last night an angel of God *whose I am* and whom I serve stood beside me and said, 'Do not be afraid, Paul. You must stand trial before Caesar....'"[274]

Paul had no doubt about who he was and whose he was. He represented an illustrious band of men and women who down the ages knew they no longer belonged to themselves or to anyone else—but to God. So Paul could declare, "I have been crucified with Christ. It is no longer I who live, but Christ who lives in me...."[275] Ownership had been renounced and transferred to Christ. This must be the starting point for understanding Paul and his leadership, in particular, as regards the matter of succession.

DISPENSABLE SCAFFOLDING

Paul never lived as if he belonged to himself, nor did he act as if any church belonged to him. When he planted a church in Ephesus and stayed on to shepherd the flock for three years, he called it "the the church of God, which he obtained with his own blood."[276] As he took leave of the church and made his way to Jerusalem, he was sure of two things: that "wolves" would arise in the church after him to savage the flock, and that opposition and imprisonment would meet him in Jerusalem. Yet he left the one, and went to the other. It was clear that for Paul, neither the church nor his life belonged to him. His over-riding passion was to do the will of God.[277]

Such a "philosophy of ministry"—if we may call it by our modern parlance—played out in his work of planting churches and appointing elders to oversee them. Roland Allen served as an Anglican missionary in China from 1895 to 1903. Reflecting on his missionary experience and researching the missionary strategy of Paul, he urged the foreign missionary to imitate the apostle.

> "He can keep ever before his mind the truth that he is there to prepare the way for the retirement of the foreign missionary. He can live his life amongst his people and deal with them *as though he would have no successor.* He should remember that he is the least permanent element in the church. He may fall sick and go home, or he may die, or he may be called elsewhere. He disappears, the church remains."[278]

First written in 1912, Allen's call went largely unheeded till some 40 years later when all missionaries were expelled from China. He had argued his case by pointing out that churches grew in Paul's absence.[279] The stay of three years in Ephesus stood out as an exception. In most cases, Paul remained long enough to appoint elders, and then moved on. In his missionary journeys, he revisited these churches. Other than such visits, he left the churches in the charge of local leaders. He did not build the ministry of the church around himself. J. Hudson Taylor, the founder of China Inland Mission, makes a similar observation:

> "I look upon foreign missionaries as the scaffolding around a rising building. The sooner it can be dispensed with, the better, or rather the sooner it can be transferred to other places to serve the same temporary use, the better."[280]

The portrait of Paul as a pioneer—going where no one had gone, and preaching the gospel where it had not been heard—conjures in our mind the image of a solitary entrepreneur. Nothing could be further from the truth. His epistles are filled with names of people: those with him at the time of writing, and those with the churches he addresses.[281] Even when he wrote to the church in Rome which he had yet to visit, he sent greetings to individuals by name. In the closing chapter of that letter, he sent greetings from eight individuals with him, and greeted 26 individuals by name, each with a brief comment.[282] The apostle valued people, remembered them by name, and believed in networking and teamwork.

ALONE, YET NOT ALONE

Following in the footsteps of Paul is modern-day church-planter and pastor Bill Hybels. In 1975, he started Willow Creek Community Church in a suburb of Chicago, meeting in a rented theatre. Since then, the church has grown to weekend services averaging 23,000, meeting on their own property of 155 acres. In addition, the church leads an association of 13,000 member churches from 90 denominations in 45 countries.[283] Willow Creek has projected Hybels to fame and many admirers may be forgiven for thinking he did it all single-handedly. Again, nothing could be further from the truth. In his book on leadership, he writes,

> "Having just turned fifty, I have recently spent a lot of time thinking about what is essential to me. I realise that there are really only two things, besides my family, that really matter to me. First, I want to do God's bidding for the rest of my life. That's primary. But in addition to that, I want to do God's bidding in authentic community with people I love and who love me."[284]

He reminisces about the years of ministry, and the team of people who has worked with him. One event illustrates the bond they share. At the end of a conference, he dismissed the crowd and walked to a corner in the backstage to pray by himself, overwhelmed by all that had taken place.

> "Several minutes passed like that, but then I realized I was not alone. The team had huddled around me with their

heads bowed. When we lifted our heads and looked at each other, it was obvious that we were all thinking the same thing: "This is as good as it gets—being powerfully used by God—*together.*"[285]

Surely, the apostle Paul would have resonated with those words. In what is believed to his last epistle from prison, Paul recalls the names of people who had worked with him, including those who had disappointed him. Demas, Crescens, Titus, Luke, Mark, Tychicus, Carpus and Alexander make up the first list of names. Prisca and Aquila, Onesiphorus, Erastus, Trophimus, Eubulus, Pudens, and Claudia, the second list.[286] John MacArthur sums up the measure of a leader's success by pointing to Paul at this stage of his life.

> "In the closing section of 2 Timothy, as Paul finished the last chapter of his final epistle—as he wrote what would literally stand as the concluding paragraph of his life— what filled the heart and mind of this great leader were the people he ministered to and worked alongside. He spoke of several individuals who had been part of his life. They were the most visible and immediate legacy of his leadership. Although he was left virtually friendless in prison, although he had been forsaken at his defense before a Roman tribunal, he was clearly *not* alone in life."[287]

TIMOTHY AND THE FOUR-MAN RELAY

Among all of Paul's co-workers, Timothy stood out. When the apostle wrote to the church in Philippi, he told his readers that he was sending to them Timothy "for I have no one like him, who will be genuinely concerned for your welfare." Paul commended Timothy to them as someone who had proven his worth, "how as a son with a father he has served with me in the gospel."[288] Timothy appears first in the Acts narrative as a disciple of Jesus in his hometown Lystra, a third generation believer with a Jewish mother and a Greek father.

He was probably converted under the ministry of Paul who calls him "my true child in the faith."[289] This could have taken place during Paul's first missionary journey. When they met again on the second journey, Acts tells us that Timothy was well-spoken of by "the brothers at Lystra and Iconium" and Paul recruited him into his team. Thus Timothy accompanied Paul on his second and third missionary journeys. For 15 years, Timothy would be Paul's companion in his travels as well as his trusted representative, sent on special missions to churches at Corinth, Thessalonica and Philippi.[290]

Timothy travelled with Paul on his much anticipated visit to Jerusalem and his perilous voyage to Rome. He featured in Paul's letters from his first imprisonment at Rome to Philemon, the Philippians, and the Colossians.[291] When Paul was released from prison, he left Timothy in Ephesus to oversee the church there. The work proved a challenge for the protégé as he was relatively young in age, timid by temperament, and poor in health. Such an unpromising leader prompts John Stott to encourage similar young leaders today.

> "...Timothy—young in years, frail in physique, retiring in disposition—who nevertheless was called to exacting responsibilities in the church of God. Greatness was being thrust upon him, and... Timothy was exceedingly reluctant to accept it. Is someone who is reading these pages in a similar situation? You are young and weak and shy, and yet God is calling you to leadership?"[292]

Despite these disadvantages working against Timothy, and perhaps because of them, Paul urged his understudy, not only to do the work, but to entrust it to others to do it: "...What you have heard from me in the presence of many witnesses entrust to faithful men who will be able to teach others also."[293] Obviously, Paul was thinking beyond himself ("from me") and his protégé Timothy ("you have heard"); he saw the third line ("faithful men") and the fourth ("others also").

In addition, there were the "many witnesses" contemporaneous with Timothy. As Paul had entrusted his legacy to Timothy, he expected Timothy to do the same. Faithful men must be found to pass on what Timothy would deposit with them. Only then would the process be duplicated and perpetuated to the fourth generation. Paul could be thinking of a four-man relay race with the baton reliably passed on from one to the other. No wonder, years after Paul was gone, the churches he founded, directly or indirectly, continued to exist and flourish.

The language Paul uses with Timothy reminds us of that used across the literary milieu of the contemporary Mediterranean world. Perry L. Stepp surveys 60 ancient Greek, Roman, Jewish and Christian texts before 200 AD on the function of succession, and identifies two "exchanges." The first is "the simple passing on of office or task or property from predecessor to successor" while the second "is seen to achieve something beyond the primary exchange."[294]

From the texts surveyed, Stepp lists the following categories in the function of succession:

1. Ensure the continuity of possession or property.
2. Ensure the continuity of manner of life.
3. Ensure the continuity of institutional vitality.
4. Ensure realization of an effect.
5. Ensure the continuity of the effect.
6. Ensure the legitimacy of the successor.[295]

Any or all of them could constitute succession of some kind. The transfer could be as basic as the handover of a piece of property or as complex as the changeover of an institution's leadership. In the case of Paul and Timothy, all the above categories, except perhaps the first, featured in the predecessor's mind.

When Paul writes to Timothy in the second letter, he gives him a solemn charge to guard the gospel, to suffer for the gospel, to persevere

in the gospel, and to preach the gospel. Timothy was called, not only
to preserve the truth of the gospel, but also to model the life of Paul in
preaching it: "Follow the pattern of the sound words that you have
heard from me, in the faith and love that are in Christ Jesus. By the
Holy Spirit who dwells within us, guard the good deposit entrusted to
you." [296] Paul passes to Timothy more than an office or a task; he gives
him an example of a life to follow.

> "So Paul's teaching is to be Timothy's guide or rule. He is
> not to depart from it. He is to follow it, better to hold it
> fast.... And he must do so 'in the faith and love which are
> in Christ Jesus'. That is, Paul is concerned not just with
> *what* Timothy is to do, but *how* he does it."[297]

MORE THAN BATON, MANTLE OR GAVEL

Succession involves more than something passed on; it calls for
someone to model a life for the successor to imitate. This is not to say
that Timothy would become another Paul—an unlikely scenario
considering the differences in their temperament and experience. But
it does mean that Timothy imbibes certain aspects of Paul's character
such as his faithfulness to his calling and willingness to suffer for the
gospel. In any case, learning never takes place in a vacuum. We not
only learn something, we learn it from someone.[298]

Though we use the analogy of a baton being passed from one
runner to another, the comparison breaks down when the baton is
seen as an inanimate object. Succession involves more than the transfer
of an object—if ever such is used, like a mantle or a gavel, it is only a
symbol. Succession goes beyond a body of knowledge passed from one
hand to another, like the company's manual or organisation's coffee
table book. No, true succession calls for wisdom gathered from
acquaintance with the predecessor and lessons drawn from observing
his or her life. Paul's life certainly had much to teach Timothy. [299]

Paul probably never thought much about the issue of ownership. But his life exemplified how ownership should play out in a legacy-rich life. Firstly, he took ownership of his calling. Twenty-five years after his encounter with Jesus on the road to Damascus, he could declare on trial before the Jewish king, "Therefore, O King Agrippa, I was not disobedient to the heavenly vision...."[300] He never forgot the day he saw Jesus and subsequently heard the call to bring the gospel to the Gentiles. Only the ownership of the calling could lead to the pursuance of it. He heard Jesus address him personally, and the commission from above became his. [301]

"Only Paul heard and understood the voice. Only Paul saw and recognised it was Jesus. None of those travelling with him received *the* vision from heaven. It was given to Paul and Paul alone. It was his vision. He made it his own. If he failed to keep it, he would be responsible, no one else."[302]

Secondly, he disclaimed ownership of his life: "But I do not account my life of any value nor as precious to myself..." This is not because he held his life cheap or worthless, for he continues, "... if only I may finish my course and the ministry that I received from the Lord Jesus, to testify to the gospel of the grace of God."[303] His life amounted to nothing if it did not fulfill his calling. He was prepared to lose his life in the line of duty. As much as he owned his calling, he disowned his life.

Finally, he transferred ownership of his ministry. The irony of ownership lies in owning and yet not owning. Paul took responsibility for the work without keeping it for himself. He owned the work without hoarding it. His life and ministry come across in a series of paradoxes: " ...as unknown, and yet well known; as dying, and behold, we live; as punished, and yet not killed; as sorrowful, yet always rejoicing; as poor, yet making many rich; as having nothing, yet possessing everything."[304] The last paradox gives us a clue to his thought about ownership. He held everything he had with an open palm. He held it as his without grasping it as *his alone* or *his always*. Thus, he had at one and the same time, everything and nothing.

THE ULTIMATE QUESTION

Such an attitude is essential to succession. Stuart Briscoe led Elmbrook Church in suburban Milwaukee, USA, for 30 years before he retired in 2000. His "Timothy" was Mel Lawrenz, associate pastor and eyewitness to his ministry for two decades. In an interview, Briscoe reflected on his succession plan.

"On John Wesley's tomb in London, it says, 'God buries his workmen, but his work goes on.' I tried to raise Elmbrook on that. As I saw my seventieth birthday approaching, I told the church: 'There are three options open to me: You can kick me out. You can carry me out. Or I can walk out.' I chose to walk out."[305]

Briscoe at 50 shared his work with Lawrenz, and at 70 stepped down, leaving a successor to continue the ministry. Thus he willingly chose to relinquish his role to another. Sooner or later, in the life of a leader, he has to confront the ultimate question: *Whose am I?* If the incumbent insists that the work belongs to him and to no one else, he will not let go of it. In the final analysis, such a leader has taken possession of what belongs to God, refusing to transfer ownership of his work or disclaim ownership of his life.

Sadly, there are leaders who have not resolved the issue of ownership. Some are bought over and owned by their benefactors. In a major denominational controversy, several leaders abstained from voting even though it was clear they should vote against an errant leader. They could not because they had benefitted from his generosity. Leaders run the risk of gifts and favours "buying" them over. Paul avoided such a danger by working with his own hands and supporting himself.

Some leaders act as if they own their followers. They need the people in order to feel good. I remember a visit to a chiropractor because of some back problem. He sat me down in his clinic, and explained his mission, "My objective is to see that you take care of your own back so that you won't have to come and see me." I was surprised and impressed: he was genuinely concerned for my health, not my money.

How many leaders will say that to their followers? If we are not weaning them from dependency on us, we are doing them and ourselves a disservice. Resolving the *Whose* question means we help each other look to God. The people do not belong to us, nor do we belong to them. We each belong to the Lord. Once we understand this, the leader is able to work himself out of the leadership position, without either party suffering dire distress.

A leader will face many questions about himself, his identity and his ability. But until he resolves the question of ownership, he is not ready for biblical leadership. Ravi Zacharias in his autobiography relates how he was once introduced in India where his father was a well-known figure. The accomplishments of Zacharias Senior were extolled in a lengthy speech, without a word said about Zacharias Junior except these, "And we will now hear from his son."[306] If we are content with such an introduction, we will have answered the ultimate question of leadership. Like the apostle Paul, we will not concern ourselves with *who* we are as long as we know *whose* we are. We will have no issue with succession.

PAUL
For Reflection and Discussion

1. In the scene from Star Wars, what finally caused Darth Vader to turn against his master, Emperor Palpatine?

2. In leadership studies, what should be the most important question? Why? How did Paul answer that question?

3. Comparing missionary practices of the last few centuries and those of Paul, what did they have in common? How did Paul avoid the mistakes made by modern missionaries who failed to see themselves as temporary and dispensable?

4. From his epistles and the names in them, we see Paul's belief in networking and teamwork. Why was this so important to him?

5. Paul viewed his protégé Timothy as part of a four-man relay. How could such a transmission of faith and leadership be implemented in our time?

Conclusion

Code of Succession: Twelve Principles

I had originally titled this last chapter "The Principles of Succession." A principle is "a law or doctrine from which others are derived." But considering the imperative mood used in each principle, these are more than laws. They call for action. I thought of *maxim* ("a general principle, serving as a rule or guide") or *axiom* ("a universally received principle"), but they signify what we believe rather than what we do. Finally, I settled for *code*, as in code of conduct ("an established set of rules for behaving in a particular situation").[310]

The danger of reading any book is to come to the end of it (or skip to the end), and think we have "got it." What that means is that we generally agree with what is written, or think that it is something that needed to be said. We may even be excited about the thought that at last something is going to be done. But until we do it, we have not got it.

Many brilliant ideas and good intentions are shipwrecked in the harbour, as were the ships of Jehoshaphat at Ezion-geber.[311] Hence, I have titled this chapter "Code of Succession" and presented it as a set of action steps. We can adopt the Code as an individual, a family or an organisation. Whether we are serious about succession—passing on our faith and our leadership to the next generation—will be seen in what we do.

Principle 1:
Cherish the heritage of our faith.

We will not pass on what we do not cherish. Jeffrey Spencer Morgan was born in 1943, some forty years after the Welsh Revival of 1904-05. His grandfather was 16 when the revival broke out, and his mother was born seven years later. The church he now attends is the granddaughter church of Moriah Church, the epicentre of the awakening. Both he and the church are two steps removed from the generation which experienced the revival. According to Morgan, the two World Wars hurt the faith of many believers. Following that, the recovering economy of the 50s and the growing prosperity of the 60s distracted them. By his generation, the heritage of the forefathers had resembled the birthright which Esau discarded for a bowl of bean soup.[307]

Unlike wine and violins, faith does not always appreciate in value with age. A better analogy is the spring: the farther it flows from the source, the muddier it becomes. To cherish our heritage, we must go back in time till we reach the place where its true value was recognised and upheld. The period of the judges need to return to the rule of the elders who in turn hark back to Joshua and Moses. No wonder the Law of Moses had to be given the second time in Deuteronomy where the catchword is: Remember. Poor successions are often the stories of bad memory. The successor forgot what made the predecessor great, and assumed that he could ride on someone else's success without paying the price.

Principle 2:
Celebrate our faith in story and music.

Asaph shows us how a legacy can last when carefully preserved and faithfully passed on. It begins in the home with our family, and comes best when packaged in story and music. We owe it to our children to give them traditions to celebrate with their children. We tell them stories and leave them memories. In our home we have a plaque over our dining table that reminds us, "Home: Where Our Story Begins." We have shelves of family albums chronicling events of each year with photos and captions. When each of our daughters turned 13, we presented her with an album of pictures of their lives, year by year. We did the same when they became adults at 21.

The church has long cherished the tradition of singing hymns and praise songs. Music helps words to stay in our memory—we remember a tune better than we recollect words. Also, a tune evokes emotions and recalls a past event subliminally, the way one picture can do what a thousand words cannot. Together, the audio and the visual are powerful tools to pack and deliver a legacy down the generations. We celebrate our faith in story and music, not only in the home but in the church community. Significant milestones must be celebrated and stories of faith must be told and retold.

Principle 3:
Think beyond our generation.

We serve our generation best when we prepare it for the next. True, we cannot know how events after us will turn out, but that is no excuse for us not to provide for it. King David provided abundantly for the building of the temple though he himself was disqualified from the actual construction of it. King Solomon benefitted from such foresight without which the temple might not have been built, at least not in such splendour. We need to think beyond our generation. As a Chinese proverb wisely observes and counsels, "One generation plants the trees under whose cool shade another generation takes its ease."

King Hezekiah did his generation a disservice by not thinking of the next. When told by the prophet Isaiah that his kingdom would be conquered and his children taken into captivity, he took comfort that it would not happen in his lifetime. Such a narrow and selfish mindset dooms the achievements in one generation to extinction.

Whether we want it or not, we are writing the next chapter by what we do or fail to do.

Principle 4:
Reckon with our mortality.

In 1984, on my first visit to India, the jeep I was travelling in met with a head-on collision with a truck on a mountain road. As the front seat passenger, I felt the full force of the impact. A few others suffered more serious injuries than I did, but we thanked the Lord our lives were spared. Later, when we saw pictures taken of the two vehicles at the accident scene, we considered it nothing short of a miracle that our jeep was not thrown off the road down the steep ravine. A clay planter I had bought as a souvenir broke into pieces in the accident. Today, put back together again, it sits in our home, reminding me that my life, like a vessel of clay, is frail and fragile.[308]

Those who do not plan for succession think they will live forever. Only two persons in the Bible knew when they would die: Jesus and Hezekiah. While Jesus spoke often of his impending death, Hezekiah lived in a state of denial. Given another 15 years to live, he did nothing to prepare for his death, and consequently bequeathed to his people the worst king in the history of the nation. Wise is the leader who reckons with his own mortality. If not death, at least the hard reality of diminishing faculties should compel us to come to terms with our eventual exit from this life. Foolish is the leader who does not prepare for what is certain to take place.

Principle 5:
Accept a role change tied to age.

Every divine directive sets out a principle and serves a purpose. The command to keep the Sabbath teaches us the rhythm of work and rest so that we may pause to worship our Creator and thus find meaning in our work. The command for the Levites to retire at fifty is a call for a role change tied to age. As a practice, it applies to the Levites; as a principle, it applies to all. How did Asaph put in place a legacy that lasted 400 years? How did the sons of Asaph and the subsequent descendants continue what he started, one generation passing the baton to the other without dropping it? The answer is twofold: Asaph was a Levite and he practised the principle of a change of role at fifty.

At fifty, he no longer did the work but handed it to younger Levites whom he went on to assist in the work—as commanded by the Lord. Thus parents pass on the work to their children, older leaders to younger ones. Those who refuse to do this are violating a principle to their own detriment. The age at which we accept and effect a role change may not necessarily be fifty. Depending on the life expectancy in different parts of the world, that age may be adjusted. But we do well to heed the words, written in 1692, found in a church in Baltimore, Maryland. "Take kindly the counsel of the years, gracefully surrendering the things of youth." If we do not accept with grace the transition from youth to middle age and learn to let go, we stand to lose it all in the end.

Principle 6:
Resist the temptation to monopolise the work.

The two great figures who appeared with Jesus at his transfiguration had one thing in common: they did not believe in succession, and thought they had to do it all alone. Moses complained that he could no longer bear the burden of leading the people. Elijah complained that he could no longer go on prophesying to the nation. Each of them felt abandoned and alone in what they did. God had to correct their thinking. For Moses, there were 70 others who could share the work with him. For Elijah, there were 7,000 who would rally around him. What made them think they were the only ones left to do the work?

Leaders may operate under the same illusion, thinking that they are the only ones who can do the work, and should therefore do it. They mark off the territory and impose sole proprietorship. Such an attitude arises from ignorance, immaturity or pride—or a combination of all these. God told Moses to look for a Joshua, and Elijah to find an Elisha. We are not alone, and should resist the temptation to monopolise what we do. Sharing our work requires forethought, effort and humility. Busy leaders who do everything must see themselves for what they are: short-sighted, lazy and proud. Then only will they delegate their work and mentor others to serve with them.

Principle 7:
Develop a mentoring culture.

This is the flipside of resisting monopoly. One is negative, the other positive. A culture takes time to foster, but when in place, allows for healthy attitudes and practices to thrive. Paul sets an example, not only as a mentor to Timothy, but as someone who encourages an environment for mentoring. Firstly, he seldom stayed long in a place after he had planted a church there. That created a vacuum for local leaders to rise to the challenge. Secondly, he built teams of co-workers wherever he went. As they looked to him as their mentor, they no doubt learned to mentor others as well. As he charged Timothy, "...What you have heard from me in the presence of many witnesses entrust to faithful men who will be able to teach others also."[309]

Paul never felt he owned the ministry for himself, neither did he built it around himself. As a result, he freely brought on board converts, disciples and colleagues to serve with him. The lists of names in his letters testify to Paul's belief in networking and team-building. How can we develop a mentoring culture? Once we have disavowed monopoly, we engage in what a church in Singapore calls "intentional disciple-making." In such a culture, every person is either a disciple or a discipler. We are either a Paul or a Timothy—in fact, we could be both, as we mentor someone and at the same time be mentored by another.

Principle 8:
Learn to let go.

Every case of good succession involves a letting go—of a position, a role or a chapter of life. Moses stood aside for Joshua to lead the people forward, Elijah took off his mantle for Elisha to put it on, and Barnabas stepped back for Paul to assume first place. But letting go is hard, and for many successful leaders the hardest part of their leadership functions. Pride may stand in the way as leaders covet the limelight. Fear may prevent them from stepping out of their comfort zone. Letting go demands more courage and humility than we imagine. It takes a man like Barnabas, described as a good man, full of the Holy Spirit's fruit of love and God's gift of faith, to do it—not once but again and again. He is like a veteran guide who takes a novice climber up a mountain, carrying his supplies and urging him on, till they reach the summit. He then lets the exhausted amateur climb the last few metres, while he holds the camera and takes pictures of him standing on top of the world.

We are born into the world with our infant hands grasping, and even as adults, we refuse to unclench them. At a seminar, the facilitator placed a 25-cent coin in a participant's hand and asked another to take it from him. They struggled, one trying to open the tight-fisted hand, the other clenching it tighter. The facilitator took over and offered a better way: he took out a five-dollar bill and held it out to the one holding the coin who immediately opened his hand to take the bill. We will find it easier to let go when we think, not of losing, but of gaining. If we will not open our hands to release, neither will we have the open hands to receive.

Paul let go of Ephesus to go to Jerusalem. On the surface, it seems like a bad bargain, leaving a church that loved him for a city that hated him. But the apostle did not consider the work his own to hoard, nor his life his own to keep. He was essentially following in the footsteps of Jesus who set his face steadfastly towards Jerusalem where the cross awaited him. Both saw the larger scheme of God's purpose, and let go of their own interests to embrace it.

Principle 9:
Navigate transitions with wisdom.

Solomon demonstrated wisdom when he took over from his father David. The way he dealt with Joab and Shimei, Adonijah and Abiathar, all of whom posed threats to his throne, showed both resoluteness and restraint. He had one of them banished, and three of them executed, two only after they failed to heed his warnings. Unfortunately, the successful transition from David to Solomon was not replicated in the handover from Solomon to Rehoboam. While the father was wise, the son proved foolish—the handling of his transition turned into a disaster, splitting the nation and sending both factions headlong towards spiritual bankruptcy.

Transitions are complex and difficult to manage. A successor has to win the confidence of the people, navigate himself out of his predecessor's shadow, and bring his team along with him. Joshua did it, so also Elisha, both of whom benefitted from the mentoring by their masters. In this regard, transitions are best anticipated by years of mentoring, since tragic accounts of bad succession are often traced to the lack of mentoring. Did Solomon ever mentor Rehoboam or Hezekiah, Manasseh?

Principle 10:
Put in place a plan for succession and stick to it.

Succession is seldom the concern of a successful leader. He has worked hard, made sacrifices, built an enterprise, and owns it. He will guard his investment with his life. A pastor, after he agreed to resign his position owing to difficulties working with the elders, was asked where he planned to worship the following Sunday. "I'm coming back here, of course," he said. "I've put in the best years of my life and I intend to protect my investment." Such an attitude is understandable, though not helpful. If this is true of someone who has stepped down, what more of an incumbent who is still holding office?

Much better it is for the leaders around the incumbent to put in place a succession plan. Many predecessors simply do not want the proposed succession to succeed because of emotional attachment and vested interests. Could this be the reason why King David did not follow through his promise to make Solomon king even when he was lying old and ill on his bed? It took Nathan the prophet in collusion with Bathsheba to remind David to act—and that, after the other son Adonijah had proclaimed himself as king. The succession plan and its implementation work best in the hands of the board or council after consultation with the incumbent. Once agreed upon, the plan should be followed through by someone other than the predecessor.

Principle 11:
Find our security in God.

Our security is found only in God. Sadly, many leaders remain insecure because they look elsewhere for security. They find it in their position and its perks, or else in people and their approval. Ironically, the most successful leaders are often the most insecure. That is because, reaching the pinnacle of success, standing where they stand, they have the most to lose should they fall or lose their place.

Consequently, insecure leaders cling on to power because their security lies in power. No succession can take place. Such leaders will not walk out on their own accord; they are either kicked out or carried out. Athaliah craved power as queen mother, seized it and abused it as queen, only to be deposed and trampled to death. Similarly, Rehoboam in grasping at power, lost it and with it, the greater part of the kingdom. We do well to ask ourselves when we feel insecure in a transition where our security lies: Honestly, is it found in God or in something else?

Principle 12:
Acknowledge the sovereignty of God.

Despite all that has been said about succession, its human intrigue and idiosyncrasy, God still reigns sovereign. Men and women may scheme and conspire, succeed by design or fail by negligence, but God's purpose eventually triumphs. Athaliah the queen infiltrated the line of David but did not remain in it for long. God kept his promise to have a son of David always on the throne till the eternal Son of David, Jesus, emerged from the long process of successions. From time to time, anonymous figures carried out divine missions without leaving their names behind.

In our study of transitions, from one person to another, or one generation to another, God's sovereign hand moves behind the scenes. While we write life's next chapter, a higher hand holds ours.

ENDNOTES

References to publications traditionally list city, country, publisher and year. With the advent of the Internet and powerful search engines, publications are easily located by author and title alone. To save space, the endnotes will list these two items, together with year and publisher (or city). Readers should have no problem finding these publications should they wish to do so.

Introduction
[1] Michael Watkins, *The First 90 Days* (Harvard Business School Press, 2003), page 1.
[2] Paul J. Meyer, *Unlocking Your Legacy* (Moody Publishers, 2002), back cover.
[3] Gen 9.12.
[4] Ex 3.6.
[5] Rev 1.11.
[6] John 21.25.
[7] Ex 20.4-6.
[8] I Cor 10.6,11.
[9] Eugene H. Peterson, *Leap Over a Wall: Earthy Spirituality for Everyday Christians* (Harper Collins, 1998), pages 3-4.

Chapter One: Moses
[10] J. Oswald Sanders, *Spiritual Leadership* (Lakeland, 1970), page 45.
[11] Eugene H. Peterson, *The Contemplative Pastor* (Word Publishing, 1989), page 27. The chapter first appeared as "The Unbusy Pastor," in *Leadership Journal* (Summer, 1981).
[12] Ex 18.13.
[13] Ex 18.14-18.
[14] Ex 18.19-21.
[15] Ex 17.8-16.

[16] I Chronicles 2.19: "When Azubah died, Caleb married Ephrath, who bore him Hur."

[17] See Ex 24.13-14 where the names of the three persons are mentioned again. Moses is taking Joshua up the mountain with him, and entrusting the people to Aaron and Hur: "And behold, Aaron and Hur are with you. Whoever has a dispute, let him go to them."

[18] Eugene Peterson gives two reasons as well: "I am busy because I am vain." "I am busy because I am lazy." The first makes me feel important, and the second lets people decide what I should do rather than deciding it myself. *The Contemplative Pastor,* pages 27-28.

[19] Ex 18.24.

[20] Ex 18.23.

[21] Num 11.4-6.

[22] Num 11.14.

[23] Num 11.16-17.

[24] Joel 2.28–29; Acts 2.16–21.

[25] Luke 10.4. ESV has "seventy-two" and indicates in the footnote that "many very old and reliable manuscripts have 'seventy-two' while many other old and reliable manuscripts have 'seventy,' and all interpreters agree that it is difficult to decide about which number was in the original of Luke's Gospel."

[26] Num 11.29.

[27] Num 27.12-13.

[28] Num 20.22-29.

[29] Num 27.16-17.

[30] Deut 1.9-13.

[31] Ex 17.9-13; 24.13 (called "assistant" the first time); 33:11.

[32] Andy Stanley, *Next Generation Leader: Five Essentials for Those Who Will Shape the Future* (Multnomah Publishers, 2003), pages 17,24.

[33] See Num 12.1-16; 16.1-40.

[34] Num 12.3.

[35] Peterson, *The Contemplative Pastor,* page 157.

Chapter Two: Joshua

[36] See www.revival-library.org; also International Revival Network at

www.openheaven.com.

[37] I am grateful to Jeffrey Spenser Morgan whose grandfather experienced the revival at the age of 16. In an email dated 2 October 2010, he notes, "The third generation after a revival is usually the one where the faith is diminished e.g. Abraham, Isaac, Esau and Jacob. Wales has become a nation of Esau's: *What good is this inheritance to me?*"

[38] Deut 31.9-13, 24-26 (Law); 19-22 (Song).

[39] Deut 31.7-8.

[40] Deut 31.20, 27.

[41] Deut 32.46-47.

[42] Josh 23.1-16.

[43] Josh 24.1-28.

[44] Josh 3.17 (cf. Ex 14.21-23); Josh 5.15 (cf. Ex 3.5); Josh 8.32 (cf. Deut 10.1-4). Here are more parallels: God was with Joshua as he was with Moses (Josh 1.5), the people pledged to obey him as they did Moses (Josh 1.17), God promised to exalt him as he did Moses (Josh 3.7), both Moses and Joshua interceded on behalf of the people (Josh 7.7; cf. Deut 9.25-29).

[45] Josh 24.28.

[46] Josh 24.29-30.

[47] Josh 13.1, 6-7.

[48] Josh 23.2; 24.1.

[49] Josh 23.15-16; 19-20. Joshua presented the situation as hypothetical: "if you transgress the covenant..., and go and serve other gods, and bow down to them.... If you forsake the LORD and serve foreign gods...."

[50] Josh 24.31; Judg 2.10-11.

[51] Judg 21.28. Also 17.6; 18.1; 19.1.

[52] Perry L. Stepp, *Leadership Succession in the World of the Pauline Circle* (Phoenix Press, 2005), page 204. See Judg 2.10-11.

[53] Stepp, *Leadership Succession*, 204. See Judg 4.1 (death of Ehud); 10.6 (death of Jair); 13.1 (death of Abdon).

⁵⁴ Josh 24.25-27 (cf. Deut 31.24-26). In both places, the Law was called to be witness against the people.

⁵⁵ Roger Steer, *Inside Story: The Story of John Stott* (Nottingham, 2009), page 149.

⁵⁶ Steer, *Inside Story*, page 150.

⁵⁷ See Lawrence M. Miller, *Barbarians to Bureaucrats: Corporate Life Cycle Strategies* (Ballatine Books, 1989). As the title suggests, the life cycle of an organisation moves from barbarians to bureaucrats, i.e. from a conquering mode to a controlling mode.

⁵⁸ Thomas L. Friedman, *The World is Flat: A Brief History of the Twenty-First Century* (Farrar, Strauss & Giroux, 2005), Updated & Expanded, 2006, page 94.

⁵⁹ Patrick Lambe, "Jetstream vs Runway Leaders" in Business Times (Singapore Press Holdings, 4 Feb 2003), quoted in Andrew Goh, *How To Pass the Torch Without Getting Burned* (Haggai Institute, 2006), pages 107-109.

⁶⁰ David W.F. Wong, The *Building of a Dream* (Singapore, 1986) chronicles the project.

Chapter Three: The Levites

⁶¹ *Far Eastern Economic Review*, 9 Nov 1989, page 40: "One curse remains: that of old men who cling on to power and cancel out many of their achievements in their dotage—from Mao Zedong to Deng Xiaoping, from Chiang Kai-shek to Sukarno, from Park Chung Hee to Kim Il Sung, from Marcos to Ne Win." See also David W.F. Wong, *Finishing Well: Closing Life's Significant Chapters* (Singapore, 2006), pages 172-173.

⁶² http://www.foreignpolicy.com/articles/2010/06/21/the_worst_of_the_worst?page=0.23.

⁶³ I Sam 12.2.

⁶⁴ NASB translates Num 8.24-25, using the word *retire*: "Men twenty-five years old or more shall come to take part in the work at the Tent of Meeting, but at the age of fifty, they must retire from their regular service and work no longer." NIV also uses the word, *retire*.

⁶⁵ Num 8:23–26

⁶⁶ Num 4.3, 47; I Chron 23.3.

[67] I Chron 23.24, 27; 2 Chron 31.17; Ezra 3.8.

[68] Katharine D. Sakenfeld, *Numbers: Journeying with God* (Eerdmans, 1995), page 53, concludes, "Scholarly explanations are nearly as numerous as the published commentaries. They include theories about periods of apprenticeship, about the need for greater maturity among the leaders, and about a scarcity of Levites or a need to limit their numbers in proportion to the priests. One or another of these theories may be historically correct, but in the absence of any textual clues, all must be regarded as speculative."

[69] I Chron 23.24-27.

[70] 2 Sam 6.1-8. Also, the two sons of Aaron, Nadab and Abihu, fell dead when they made offerings unacceptable to God (Num 3.3).

[71] The upper limit is also implied in Num 4.3,29,35,42,47 where "from thirty years old up to fifty years old" describes all those listed.

[72] See 1 Chron 23.24–32.

[73] *The Pulpit Commentary: 1 Chronicles*, ed. H. D. M. Spence-Jones (Logos Research Systems, 2004; first published by Funk & Wagnalls,1880), pages 381-82. Matthew Henry, *Matthew Henry's Commentary on the Whole Bible: Complete and Unabridged in One Volume* (Hendrickson, 1996), on 1 Chron 23.24–32. Risto Nurmela titles his book, *The Levites: Their Emergence as a Second-Class Priesthood* (Scholars Press, 1998).

[74] The support the Levites provided became a long-standing tradition, so that, more than 300 years later, when Josiah reinstated the Passover, it is recorded that "the Levites made preparations for themselves, and for the Aaronic priests." In addition, we read, "The gatekeepers at each gate did not need to leave their posts, because their fellow Levites made preparations for them." 2 Chron 35.14-15.

[75] I Chron 23.28-29.

[76] I Chron 23.30.

[77] See chapter on Asaph in this book.

[78] Num 8.5-11 (Levites); Lev 8.30-36 (priests).

[79] Philip J. Budd, *Word Biblical Commentary*, Vol. 5, *Numbers* (Word Books, 1984), 94.

[80] Num 8.14-19. Note the terms used by Raymond Brown to describe the Levites as they were set apart "by the laying of hands, and so designated to serve as substitutes on behalf of the other tribes. Whenever they functioned as associates and partners with the priesthood, they were doing their work in the place of others." *Bible Speaks Today, Numbers* (Inter-Varsity Press, 2002), page 68.

[81] See Num 18.20–24; 26.62; Deut 10.9; 18.1,2; Josh 18.7.The fact that the Levites did not own land is consistently stated through the narratives.

[82] Num 18.20.

[83] Num 35.6-8.

[84] Matthew Henry, on Num 8.5–26.

[85] John F. Walvoord & Roy B. Zuck, *The Bible Knowledge Commentary: An Exposition of the Scriptures* (Victor Books, 1983), Num 8:20–26.

[86] Num 8.25-26.

[87] Steven L. McKenzie, *1-2 Chronicles, Abingdon* OT Commentaries (Abingdon, 2004), 194, notes that "army" is used of the service of the Levites (Num 4.3,23,30,35); the reference "may have arisen from the function of the Levites as a security force for the temple precincts."

[88] James L. Synder, *In Pursuit of God: The Life of A. W. Tozer* (Christian Publications, 1991), pages 216-217.

Chapter Four: Asaph

[89] I Chron 6.39.

[90] I Chron 15.16-19.

[91] I Chron 16.4-7. Italics added.

[92] I Chron 16.39-42.

[93] I Chron 25.1-31. The list of numerous names ranges, as we would say, from Azarel to Zeri.

[94] I Chron 25.6-8.

[95] Num 8.23-26. See chapter on the Levites.

[96] I am grateful to Selena Hia for first bringing this to my attention and referring me to "The Future Of Worship" delivered by Bob Kauflin at the 2009 WorshipGod Conference. At her suggestion, I

visited www.sovereigngraceministries.org and received from Chelsea Kauflin the cited article by Don DeVries.

[97] 2 Chron 5.12-14.

[98] 2 Chron 20.5,13.

[99] 2 Chron 20.14.

[100] 1 Chron 25.1-2.

[101] See I Sam 10.5 where a group of prophets were prophesying "with harp, tambourine, flute, and lyre."

[102] 2 Chron 20.21-22.

[103] 2 Chron 29.12-15

[104] 2 Chron 33.1-9.

[105] 2 Chron 35.15.

[106] Ezra 2.41. Nehemiah 7.44 likewise mentions the presence of the sons of Asaph but gives the number as 148.

[107] Neh 11.15-18.

[108] Neh 12.35. Listed as someone who played the trumpet at the dedication of the wall of Jerusalem was "Zechariah son of Jonathan, the son of Shemaiah, the son of Mattaniah, the son of Micaiah, the son of Zaaur, the son of Asaph" (Neh 12.25). At the foundation-laying of the temple, the sons of Asaph played the cymbals (Ezra 3.10).

[109] Ezra 3.11. Compare: "For he is good, for his steadfast love endures forever" (2 Chron 5.13).

[110] Psalms 50, 73-83.

[111] Psalm 78.65. ESV translates: "as from sleep, like a strong man shouting because of wine."

[112] Psalm 78:4–6.

[113] Paul J. Meyer, *Unlocking Your Legacy* (Moody Publishers, 2002), page 19.

[114] I Chron 25.1. Translated as "chiefs of the service" in ESV, but most translations prefer the military terms: "captains of the host" (KJV), "captains of the army" (NKJV), "the commanders of the army" (NIV).

[115] 2 Chron 35.15 tells us that they were "at their stations according to the command of David" (NASB), or "in the places prescribed by David" (NIV).

[116] Psalm 78.4.

Chapter Five: David

[117] See Ignatius Wibowo, "Leadership Succession and Its Impact on the Party's Rank and File," *China's Post-Jiang Leadership Succession: Problems and Perspectives* (Singapore University Press, 2002), ed. John Wong & Zheng Yongnian, pages 119-138.

[118] Acts 13:36–37.

[119] John Edmund Haggai, *Serve Your Generation!* (Haggai Institute, 2010). I first heard the statements in a convocation message in Maui, Hawaii, in March 1997.

[120] I Chron 17.1.

[121] I Chron 17.4,10. Two reasons were given for the divine denial of David's request: God had never asked for a house to dwell in, and David as a man of war was disqualified from building such a house.

[122] I Chron 17.11-12.

[123] I Chron 22.2-4.

[124] I Chron 17.16-17.

[125] I Chron 22.5.

[126] The ESV Study Bible (Crossway Bibles, 2008), page 719, compares I Kings and I Chronicles and gives a list of what is included and excluded between them. Omitted from I Chronicles are: David's adultery with Bathsheba and murder of Uriah, Amnon's rape of Tamar, Absalom's rebellion, Adonijah's bid for kingship, Solomon's threatened succession, and his sins of polygamy and idolatry.

[126a] Eugene H. Peterson, *Leap Over a Wall* (Harper Collins, 1997), page 9.

[127] Matthew Henry, *Matthew Henry's Commentary on the Whole Bible* (Hendrickson, 1996), 1 Kings 1:1–4.

[128] 2 Sam 3.2-5. See also 2 Chron 14.3-7 for another list of sons and daughters born to David after he moved from Hebron to Jerusalem. Solomon is mentioned in this second list.

[129] Described as a very handsome man, Adonijah appeared in public with horses and chariots and 50 men as outriders to make known his ambition and claim to the throne. "His father had never at any time displeased him by asking, 'Why have you done thus and so?'" (I Kings 1.5-6).

[130] See "Closing a Chapter of Grief," in *Finishing Well: Closing Life's Significant Chapters* (Singapore, 2006) for a study of how David reacted at the death of each of his sons: Bathsheba's son, Amnon, and Absalom.

[131] I Kings 2.9.

[132] I Kings 2.1-9.

[133] http://en.wikipedia.org/wiki/Spanish_Succession_War

[134] The apostle Paul in listing the qualifications of a leader asks the rhetorical question: "...if someone does not know how to manage his own household, how will he care for God's church?" (I Tim 3.5).

[135] E. R. Thiele, "Coregencies and Overlapping Reigns among the Hebrew Kings," *Journal of Biblical Literature* 93 (1974), pages 174–200, points to the reigns of Omri with Tibni, Jehoram with Jehoshaphat, and Jotham with Azariah.

[136] Gene Rice, *Nations Under God: A Commentary on the Book of I Kings* (Grand Rapids, 1990), page 17.

Chapter Six: Solomon

[137] *Diodorus of Sicily,* The Loeb Classical Library, translated by C. Bradford Welles, Vol.8, pages 466-467; Vol.9, pages 19-21. See also Perry L. Stepp, *Leadership Succession in the World of the Pauline Circle* (Sheffield, 2005), page 31.

[138] Eccl 2.18–19.

[139] I Kings 2.5-6, 8-9.

[140] I Kings 2.1-9.

[141] I Kings 2.28-46.

[142] I Kings 2.26-27 (Abiathar), 13-25;19-27 (Adonijah).

[143] I Kings 2.46.

[144] Geoffrey W. Bromiley, *The International Standard Bible Encyclopedia, Revised* (Eerdmans, 2002), Vol. IV, page 568.

[145] 2 Sam 16.11-12.

[146] 2 Sam 19.16-23; I Kings 2.8.
[147] M.P. Matheney considers it "not an expression of personal vengeance" but "rather the satisfaction of a primitive idea of the danger to the dynasty of unavenged innocent blood." See his commentary on I Kings in Broadman Bible Commentary (Nashville, 1970), Vol. 3, page 163.
[148] 2 Sam 21.6-9
[149] I Kings 3.7–9
[150] I Kings 6.38-7.1.
[151] I Kings 11.14-43.
[152] For more parallels from the lives of Hadad, Rezon and Jeroboam, see Peter J. Leithart, I & 2 Kings, Brazos Theological Commentary on the Bible (Grand Rapids, 2006), pages 87-88.
[153] I Sam 13.14. God rejects Saul, forfeits his kingdom, and chooses David as a man after his own heart.
[154] 1 Kings 11.26–40.
[155] I Kings 11.29-39.
[156] I Kings 11.4, 7, 10-11.
[157] I Kings 12.28–32
[158] E. G. 1 Kings 16:26 (Omri), 16.31 (Ahab); 2 King 3.3 (Jehoram), 15.28 (Pekah).
[159] Os Guinness, The Gravedigger File: Papers on the Subversion of the Modern Church (Inter-Varsity Press, 1983), page 15: "The underlying strategy of Operation Gravedigger is as stark in its simplicity as it is devastating in its results. It may be stated like this: 'Christianity contributed to the rise of the modern world; the modern world, in turn, has undermined Christianity; Christianity has become its own gravedigger.'"
[160] I Kings 11.4.
[161] Eccl 7.8.
[162] C.S. Lewis, The Screwtape Letters (Geoffrey Bles, 1942), page 143.

Chapter Seven: Elijah

[163] Basil Mathews, John R. Mott: World Citizen (Harper & Brothers Publishers, 1934), page 397.

[164] Job 38.4.

[165] 1 Kings 19.11-13.

[166] Luke 9.30-31.

[167] 1 Kings 19.4, 10.

[168] 1 Kings 19.15-18.

[169] 2 Kings 2.9-10; Deut 21.17.

[170] 2 Kings 3.11.

[171] 2 Kings 2.16–17.

[172] I Kings 19.15-16.

[173] 2 Kings 8.7-15; 2 Kings 9.1-10.

[174] 2 Kings 9.1, 4,6.

[175] Carson Pue, *Mentoring Leaders: Wisdom for Developing Character, Calling and Competence* (Grand Rapids, 2005), page 62. Nothing grows under the banyan tree not only from the lack of rain, but also the lack of sunlight.

[176] G. Rawlinson, "II Kings," *The Pulpit Commentary* (Grand Rapids, 1950), page 20.

[177] "Henrich Bullinger, *Wikipedia,* posted 6 September 2010.

[178] I Kings 21.19-24.

[179] I Kings 21.17-29 (Elijah's prophecy), I Kings 22.29-38 (Ahab's death), 2 Kings 9.30-37 (Jezebel's death).

[180] 2 Kings 2.12 (Elisha to Elijah); 13.14 (Joash to Elisha).

[180a] J. Oswald Sanders, *Spiritual Leadership* (Lakeland, 1967), page 134.

[181] For lists of miracles by Elijah and by Elisha (11 each), see W. Graham Scroggie, *The Unfolding Drama of Redemption* (Pickering & Inglis, 1963), Vol. 1, pages 332-333: "Three of Elijah's, and one of Elisha's miracles were of judgment, and the remainder, eight, and ten, were of mercy, and providence.".

[182] 2 Kings 2.14.

[183] 2 Kings 2.15.

[184] A pastor I know gives this book to all new staff joining the church: Michael Watkins, *The First 90 Days: Critical Success Strategies for New Leaders at All Levels* (Harvard Business School Press, 2003).

[185] 2 Kings 2.10.

Chapter Eight: Hezekiah

[186] French, Italian and Japanese proverbs respectively. See Wolfgang Miedler, *The Prentice-Hall Encyclopedia of World Proverbs* (Prentice-Hall, 1986).

[187] 2 Chron 28.1-2 (Ahaz); 29.2 (Hezekiah); 33.2 (Manasseh).

[188] 2 Kings 17.7-23 gives the reasons why Israel fell, beginning with these words: "And this occurred because the people of Israel had sinned against the LORD their God, who had brought them up out of the land of Egypt from under the hand of Pharaoh king of Egypt, and had feared other gods."

[189] 2 Kings 18.14.

[190] "Rabshakeh" is a title more than a name, variously translated "field commander" (NIV), "chief adviser" (NET) and "chief of staff" (NLT).

[191] 2 Chron 32.9–15.

[192] 2 Kings 19.3-4.

[193] 2 Kings 16.8–13

[194] 2 Kings 19.7.

[195] 2 Kings 20.14–19.

[196] 2 Chron 32.31.

[197] Randy Pausch, *The Last Lecture* (Hyperion, 2008), page 191. He died on 25 July 2008.

[198] 2 Chron 33.12–13

[199] Prov 22.6.

[200] Timothy Tow, *John Sung My Teacher* (Singapore, 1985), pages 73, 88-89.

[201] Henry T. & Richard Blackaby, *Experiencing God Day-By-Day* (Broadman & Holman Publishers, 1998), page 282.

[202] 2 Kings 20.1-11; also Isa 38.1-8, 21-22. Hezekiah did not ask for more time, but it was implied in his plea.

Chapter Nine: Bathsheba

[203] David W. F. Wong, *Make Them Laugh, Help Them Learn* (Singapore, 2002), page 14.

[204] Roger N. Whybray, *The Succession Narrative: A Study of II Samuel 9-20; I Kings 1 and 2* (Alec R. Allenson, 1968), page 40. According to

him, Bathsheba is a "minor character" made use of by men: David used her for lust, Nathan used her for political ends, and Adonijah used her for romantic designs.

[205] 2 Sam 11.1-27.

[206] David had married six wives prior to marrying Bathsheba. Of David's 19 sons, four were born to Bathsheba (not including the nameless child who died in infancy): Shimea, Shobab, Nathan and Solomon. See I Chron 3.1-9.

[207] Edith Deen, *All the Women of the Bible* (Harper & Row, 1955), page 117. See Prov 2.12-18 and 31.10-31.

[208] I Kings 2.17.

[209] See 2 Sam 16:20–22. Absalom was advised to take David's concubines, and make it public he had done so. This would strengthen his position as he sought to usurp his father's throne.

[210] Paul R. House, vol. 8, *1, 2 Kings*, electronic ed., Logos Library System; The New American Commentary (Broadman & Holman Publishers, 2001), pages 99–100.

[211] 1 Kings 2.22, *The Message*.

[212] Commentary on I Kings 11.26: Jerome T. Walsh, *I Kings: Studies in Hebrew Narrative and Poetry* (Collegeville, Minnesota, 1996), pages 142-143.

[213] 2 Chron 22.3: "He [Ahaziah] also walked in the ways of the house of Ahab, for his mother [Athaliah] was his counselor in doing wickedly." See also 2 Chron 21.4, and 2 Chron 24.7 where she is called "that wicked woman."

[214] 2 Chron 23.12-15.

[215] Deen, *All the Women of the Bible* , 142.

[216] See http://en.wikipedia.org/wiki/Cleopatra_VII

[217] See http://en.wikipedia.org/wiki/Empress_Dowager_Cixi.

[218] See http://en.wikipedia.org/wiki/Jospehine Bonaparte.

[219] Robin Gallaher Branch, *Jeroboam's Wife: The Enduring Contributions of the Old Testament's Least-Known Women* (Hendrickson, 2009), page 93.

[220] Matt 20.20-28 has the mother asking the favour, whereas Mark 10.35-40 has James and John making the request. It is likely that the idea came from the mother, with the sons concurring with it.

[221] Num 12.2. See also Num 11.16-17.

[222] Exod 15.20-21.

Chapter Ten: Peter

[223] "Poland mourns president, elite killed in crash" by Gareth Jones & Lidia Kelly, posted on Reuters, 11 April 2010.

[224] Mark 8.31; 9.9.

[225] Matt 16.17-19.

[226] John 1.42

[227] Michael Green, *The Message of Matthew* (Inter-Varsity Press, 2000), page 179

[228] Matt 16.13-23.

[229] Howard Behar, *It's Not About the Coffee: Leadership Principles from a Life at Starbucks* (Penguin Group, 2007), page 141.

[230] See Mark 9.5-7 which also tells us, "For he did not know what to say, for they were terrified."[231] Matt 26.31-35, 69-75.

[232] An example is Luke 22.31-32 where Jesus uses the plural "you" to address the disciples (v. 31), and the singular "you" for Peter (v. 32), together in the same saying. Likewise in Mark 8.33, Jesus looks at the disciples and addresses Peter.

[233] Luke 24.34; I Cor 15.5; Mark 16.7.

[234] See "Peter: Full Circle" in David W. F. Wong, *Journeys Beyond the Comfort Zone* (Singapore, 2001), 97-107.

[235] Mark 4.35-41; 9.33-34; 8.14-21.

[236] MaryKate Morse, *Making Room for Leadership: Power, Space and Influence* (Inter-Varsity Press, 1998), page 151.

[237] Mark 1.35-38

[238] A. B. Bruce, *The Training of the Twelve* (Kregel Publications, 1971), page 41. The book was first published in 1871.

[239] Mark 5.37; 9.2; 14.33.

[240] Mark 9.33-34. Even James and John, already in the inner circle, vied for the top two positions (Mark 10.35-41).

[241] Mark 4.10 and 13.3 have the Twelve and the Three (respectively) speaking with Jesus in private. Mark 4.35-41 and 6.45-52 have the disciples in their boat facing danger; each time, Jesus appeared to have left the disciples on their own.

[242] Matt 26.31-32.

[243] John 10.11-14.

[244] John Edmund Haggai, *The Leading Edge: The Haggai Institute Story* (Kobrey Books, 1999), pages 8-9.

[245] John 10.11-13.

[246] I am grateful to Clive Lim for these thoughts. His doctoral work on leadership focuses on Chinese entrepreneurship in Singapore.

[247] Peter urges his fellow-elders to "shepherd the flock *of God*" (italics added) and look forward to a reward from "the chief Shepherd" (I Pet 5.1-4). Jesus' commission to him was "Feed my sheep" not "Feed *your* sheep" (John 21.17).

Chapter Eleven: Barnabas

[248] Richard Stengel, *Mandela's Way: Fifteen Lessons on Life, Love, and Courage* (Crown Publishers, 2009), page 201.

[249] Cited by Stengel. Ramaphosa, born 1952, is a South African lawyer, trade union leader, activist, politician and businessman.

[250] Stengel, *Mandela's Way*, pages 201-202.

[251] Up till the departure from Cyprus, Luke consistently places Barnabas' name first, and thereafter Paul's name (Acts 13.43, 46, 50; 15.2, 22, 35). The exceptions are Acts 15.12, 25 (at the Jerusalem Council) and Acts 14.14 (at Lystra, probably following the order of the deities).

[252] Acts 4.36.

[253] Acts 9:26-28

[254] Gal 1.11-24. John Stott, *The Message of Galatians* (Inter-Varsity Press, 1968), page 34, cites a suggestion that "those three years in Arabia were a deliberate compensation for the three years of instruction which Jesus gave the other apostles, but which Paul missed."

[255] *Paul of Tarsus*, starring Johannes Brandrup, directed by Roger Young, and shot in Morocco in 2000. It is distributed by www.innoform.com.sg.

[256] F. F. Bruce, *Commentary on the Book of Acts* (Marshall, Morgan & Scott, 1962), page 207.

[257] Acts 9.31.

[258] Acts 11.19-21.

[259] C. Peter Wagner, *Lighting the World* (Regal Books, 1995), page 95. The book is second in the series, *The Acts of the Holy Spirit*, by Wagner.

[260] The word is "Hellenists", a term describing people who imbibe the Greek culture and/or speak the Greek language. Since it is used here in contrast to "Jews", it refers to Gentiles.

[261] F. F. Bruce, "Acts" in *The New Bible Commentary Revised*, edited by Donald Guthrie, et al. (Inter-Varsity Press, 1970), page 986.

[262] Acts 11.22. Similarly, when Philip preached the gospel among the Samaritans, the Jerusalem church sent Peter and John to investigate (Acts 8.14).

[263] Acts 11.23-24.

[264] Acts 13.13 (italics added): "Now *Paul and his companions* set sail from Paphos and came to Perga in Pamphylia. And John left them and returned to Jerusalem...." The team started as "Barnabas and Saul".

[265] Acts 13.44-46.

[266] Acts 14.21-23.

[267] See chapter on Paul and Timothy in this book.

[268] Acts 13.13.

[269] See Acts 15.10-21. Peter: "...Why are you putting God to the test by placing a yoke on the neck of the disciples that neither our fathers nor we have been able to bear? But we believe that we will be saved through the grace of the Lord Jesus, just as they will." James: "Therefore my judgment is that we should not trouble those of the Gentiles who turn to God..."

[270] 2 Tim 4.11.

[271] Col 4.10; Philem 24. See also I Pet 5.13 where Mark is mentioned by Peter.

[272] Timothy Keller, The *Prodigal God: Recovering the Heart of the Christian Faith* (Hodder & Stoughton, 2008), pages xiv-xv.

Chapter Twelve: Paul

[273] See David W. F. Wong, 'The Whose of Leadership: The Ultimate Question of Leadership,' in *Understanding the Modern World Through Christian Eyes* (Malaysia: Kairos Research Centre, June 2007), pages 3-5.

[274] Acts 27.22-24, NIV, italics added.

[275] Gal 2.20.

[276] Acts 20.28.

[277] Acts 20.17-38. See fuller treatment of this in David W. F. Wong, *Finishing Well: Closing Life's Significant Chapters* (Singapore, 2006), pages 165-175.

[278] Roland Allen, *Missionary Methods: St. Paul's or Ours?* (Eerdmans, 1962), page 153.

[279] Allen, *Missionary Methods*, page 103, cited Col 2.1, noting, "...we know by name at least one organized church of which St Paul himself says that he had not seen the members."

[280] Source unknown.

[281] The letter to the Ephesians is the only exception with no personal names mentioned. This could be because it was a circular letter, copied and sent to several churches. See John R. W. Stott, *The Message of the Ephesians* (Inter-Varsity Press, 1979), pages 23-24.

[282] Rom 16.3-16, 21-24.

[283] http://en.wikipedia.org/wiki/Willow_Creek_Community_Church posted 21 Oct 2010.

[284] Bill Hybels, *Courageous Leadership* (Zondervan, 2002), page 76.

[285] Hybels, *Courageous Leadership*, page 79.

[286] 2 Tim 4.10-13, 19-21.

[287] John MacArthur, *The Book on Leadership* (Nelson Books, 2004), page 184.

[288] Phil 2.19-23.

[289] I Tim 1.2.

[290] Acts 16.1-5; I Thess 3.1-6; I Cor 4.17; Acts 20.1-15

[291] Acts 20.1-4; Philem 1, Phil 1.1; Col 1.1.

[292] John R. W. Stott, *The Message of 2 Timothy* (Inter-Varsity Press, 1973), page 20.

[293] 2 Tim 2.2.

[294] Perry L. Stepp, *Leadership Succession in the World of the Pauline Circle*, page 192.

[295] Stepp, *Leadership Succession*, pages 193-194, explains (4) as "an *effect* that is *succession-dependent*, one which began under the predecessor and was finally realized under the successor" while (5) focuses on "an *effect/result which is shared by the predecessor and the successor* but the realization of which is not dependent upon the succession."

[296] 2 Tim 1.13-14.

[297] Stott, *The Message of 2 Timothy*, page 44.

[298] So Paul in 2 Tim 3.14 charges Timothy, not only to continue in "what you have learned", but also to remember "from whom you learned it."

[299] In 2 Tim 3.10-11, Paul recounts his Life and points to his "persecutions and sufferings that happened at Antioch, at Iconium,and at Lystra." The last city was Timothy's hometown (Acts 16.1-2), and it is probable that Timothy knew about the stoning of Paul, and perhaps even witnessed it.

[300] Acts 26.19.

[301] "Saul, Saul...." (Acts 9.4; 22.7), prior to his change of name to Paul.

[302] David W. F. Wong, *Journeys Beyond the Comfort Zone* (Singapore, 2001), pages 114-115. Those travelling with Paul heard some sound but did not see anyone (Acts 9.7); they saw a bright light, but did not understand the voice speaking to Paul (Acts 22.9).

[303] Acts 20.24.

[304] 2 Cor 6.9-10.

[305] Stuart Briscoe in an interview at a "Leadership Forum" hosted by Christianity Today, posted 1 July, 2004.See http://www.christianitytoday.com/le/2003/summer/1.24.html?start=5&sms_ss=email.

[306] Ravi Zacharias, *Walking from East to West* (Zondervan, 2006), page 34.

[307] I am grateful to Spencer for his thoughts in an email of 2 Oct 2010.

[308] See 2 Cor 4.7.

[309] 2 Tim 2.2.

[310] Chambers 20th Century Dictionary (W & R Chambers, 1983).

[311] I Kings 22.49.

AFTERWORD

Authors wonder whether readers read Foreword, so some have resorted to writing Afterword. Also, after all is said and written in a book, not all is said and written. So I take this opportunity to answer some questions and relate personal experiences, both mine and those of friends who kindly shared their succession stories with me.

LEGACY AND FAMILY

You said that all of us will leave behind a legacy. The question is whether it will be a good legacy or a bad one. What is a good legacy, and a bad one?

A good legacy should include two things. Firstly, our faith in God is passed on to the next generation. Secondly, our work continues and grows with our departure. To these, we may add a third: Our name is a blessing to those who remember us. In contrast, a bad legacy is when our faith in God dies with us, our work falters, stagnates or collapses with our departure, and our name makes little or no positive impact on those who remember us.

In practical terms, how do we pass on our faith?

As a father, my children need to see my commitment to God, and the practice of my faith. As a leader, my followers need to see the same. I may not be perfect, but I must be consistent and faithful over the long haul. As I study the lives of great leaders, the ones whose legacies have made the greatest impact are those who matched their lives to their teachings, and did so to the end.

Our children and followers are quick to see inconsistency in our lives. The way we treat our spouse or our colleagues makes lasting impressions on them. The greatest gift we can give our children is our love for our spouse demonstrated in everyday living. Parents need to be careful what they do in the presence and hearing of their children. If we make unkind remarks about the pastor or critical comments about the church, our children pick them up. No wonder some of them grow up thinking the church is a sham and all Christians are hypocrites.

What if, after all we have done, our children go astray from the Lord?

Firstly, there is no point in tormenting ourselves with guilt. If we have failed in any way as parents, let us confess it and accept God's forgiveness—and no more revisit our failures. Secondly, we should never stop praying for our wayward children to return to the Lord— even when they turn adults. Remember how even Manasseh, the worst king of a godly father, turned to the Lord in the end. There is always hope as long as we live.

I remember listening to the testimony of James Dobson, the founder of "Focus on the Family" and one of America's most influential public leaders. His great-grandfather came to the Lord and prayed for his family. God gave him a promise that for the next four generations, God would raise someone in each generation to serve him. Dobson was the son, grandson and great-grandson of pastors. That prayer of more than a century ago was answered.[1] That is the power of prayer!

What do you say to parents who give their lives to their careers and "outsource" their parenting to domestic maids and grandparents?

I would say that parenting cannot be outsourced. Domestic maids are helpful when it comes to taking care of needs such as cooking and cleaning, but not parenting. Even grandparents need to be careful not to take that over. When our daughter had her first baby, my wife flew to the USA and spent more than a month with her. Let me quote what our daughter wrote as a tribute for a Mother's Day event:

"Two days before the birth you said to me that you would help only with laundry, ironing, cleaning and cooking, but would leave the mothering of the newborn solely to me. You said to me, 'You planned for this baby, my baby days are over, so you take care of your baby—that's not my job!' I was initially stunned, and a little puzzled, wondering why you wouldn't want to help. But looking back, you were wise in that decision. You were helping me learn to be a mother, by doing the housework, you cleared the way for me to launch on the steep learning curve of motherhood."[2]

Does it mean that the mother should always be a homemaker?

Not necessarily. It depends on her work outside the home. If she works regular hours and does not take work home, she could still give quality time to her child. Alternatively, she could work from home, and allocate hours for work and time for her child. I am blessed to be married to a kindergarten teacher. Each time when our daughters were born, she stopped work and spent much time with them. When each was old enough, my wife went back to work in the kindergarten and took our daughter with her. Our daughters have grown and made us proud—I attribute it to those early days when my wife spent both quantity and quality time with them.

Does the husband have a role to play too?

Of course, the father figure in the lives of our children is more important than we realise. He may be the primary provider in terms of finances, but every child looks to the father for his time and his love. In my book *Finishing Well*, I related a story that illustrates this point. A friend of mine travels a lot in his work. Each trip he would bring home a toy train for his son who loved trains. One day, as he got ready to go on yet another trip, he asked the son, "What kind of train do you want Daddy to buy for you this time?" The son replied, "Daddy, if you don't have to buy trains for me, will you stay at home?"[3]

It is clear that the presence of the father was more important to the young child than any present he could buy for him. When we work hard at our jobs, put in long hours, spend days away from our family, and say we do it "for the sake of our children"—we may need to ask if that is what they want or need.

What if a couple cannot afford to live on one income?

I advise couples when they marry to budget on the basis on one income. Should one of them stop work, by choice or circumstances, they would still be able to meet their expenses, including loan repayments. Decisions on housing and other major expenses that involve loans should be carefully weighed. We make decisions and these decisions in turn make us. For example, a couple who make financial commitments based on the future earnings of both of them are painting themselves into a corner. Better to start small, and build up their assets before they take on more financial challenges.

Each one of us has to decide our "chosen lifestyle"—where we live, how we live and most importantly, why. We need to resist the subtle pressures of the world to conform to a lifestyle motivated by pride and status. Advertisements that appeal to prestige, class, and exclusive ownership should be viewed with suspicion. We need to challenge the message of the world that life consists in the abundance of things we acquire. If we are interested in the legacy we leave behind, w should focus on relationships rather than on things.

LIFESTYLE AND LEGACY

Would you therefore advocate a "simple lifestyle"?

Yes, that was one of the key issues discussed at the Lausanne Congress of World Evangelisation in 1974. I attended a follow-up consultation in 1980 which issued a fuller statement on the subject.[4]

Since "simple" is relative in different parts of the world, the call is perhaps for a "simpler" lifestyle. We could simplify our lives without too much pain or grief, especially in affluent nations. In any case, as we grow past mid-life, we reach a point when we realise that we can take nothing with us when we die.

I once heard my good friend Phineas Dube, elder stateman from Zimbabwe, share how he wanted to die empty. I knew he didn't mean to die bankrupt. What he meant was that by the time he dies, he would have passed on to others all that is on his heart, in his mind, in his hands. I resonated with that. When I started my term as a leadership mentor of a church, I asked the staff what they expected of me. One of the younger ones said, "Tell us all the stories of your life." To leave a legacy, we need to empty ourselves. Not only to tell our stories and communicate our passion, but also to diminish our possessions.

The idea of "dying empty" seems to tie in well with passing on the torch. Could the reason why leaders avoid talk of succession be because they would not let go?

Definitely. Our natural tendency in life is to acquire things— both tangible and non-tangible—and hold on to them. That is why some leaders are reluctant to step down once they occupy a position. The sad thing is that these leaders often have done a lot of good in their earlier years. But by holding on, they outlive their usefulness, and become a liability.

As this book was being written, we witnessed the dramatic events in Egypt when street protests by hundreds of thousands of ordinary people brought down President Hosni Mubarak. In 18 days of unprecedented uprising, 30 years of his rule were brought to an ignominious end. The story could have been different if a viable succession plan had been put in place, and the leader, still respected and loved, stepped down graciously and honourably.

How does one know when it is time to step down? What was your experience?

Firstly, we should consider stepping down when we feel that we have taken the church or organisation as far as we can. In other words, we have reached a maintenance mode and are simply marking time. Some symptoms of such a stage are the lack of challenge and the loss of passion. It may take others to see these symptoms in us.

In some cases, there may already be someone in the wings ready to take over, and bring the work to the next level. If not, we should start looking for one. I was blessed to have two associate pastors capable of taking over from me when my wife noted that I was going to bed earlier and apparently having less to do. I was feeling restless and looking for another challenge.

The situation was different in my second position. I was promoted to a role which became increasingly administrative. I was reminded of something I learned in school. Known as *The Peter Principle*, it says, "In a hierarchy, every employee tends to rise to his level of incompetence."[5] I felt this was what was happening in my case. I had started as the director of a training institute where I was involved in the training of leaders. My wife and I lived on-site at the training centre and were with the participants in and out of the seminar rooms, at meals, and on weekends when we took them to church.

In my new role, we moved out of the centre and I found myself several steps removed from the training sessions. Though I had responsibility for the training in both Maui and Singapore, I found myself spending more time in planning, travelling, writing reports, meetings, budgetting, staffing, and so on. That was when I felt it was time to step aside for someone else. So another indication for stepping down could be when we are doing what we no longer feel competent to do and fulfilled in doing.

Should we leave a position because we are unhappy with it?

Unhappiness with a position or role may prompt us to consider leaving, but we should never leave any place with unhappiness—either on our part or the part of those left behind. I have known those who had left with unresolved conflicts and hurt feelings—they simply brought their unhappiness to the next place. Difficult though it sounds, we should stay till conflicts are resolved, forgiveness is released and peace is restored before we move on. Relationships are important, and we should close each chapter as friends. Preferably, we should leave a place when all is well, not when things are bad.

RETIREMENT AND SENSE OF HONOUR

You mentioned that the reluctance to retire may be traced to a wrong concept of service, that is, service for God must be from the position we hold. You said that we can still serve God when we step down and assume another role, with or without a position. It sounds good, but what are the practical implications?

There are two practical implications. The first is financial. If a leader is dependent on a position for regular income, stepping down from it means the loss of income. If he has dependents to support and debts to repay, such a decision is difficult. The second is vocational. If he steps out of a position, what does he step into? Is there any meaningful role or gainful employment left for him? The fear of an uncertain, insecure future makes retirement a frightening prospect.

What can the leader do in such situations?

Firstly, as a responsible person, a leader has to plan and handle his finances well. The ideal is for him to become financially free by a certain age, that is, when all his debts are cleared. This means he has to exercise care and caution in the loans he acquires on his house, car, studies, business, and so on. Returning outstanding loans becomes a priority in financial management. I have found great value in having a financial consultant track me and my wife over the years and advise us on our finances.

Once that is taken care of, vocational change becomes less problematic. Hopefully, by retirement age, dependents are less, and financial needs more manageable. In some cases, we may have to downsize our expectations and simplify our lifestyle. I believe that if we have been faithful to the Lord, he will not fail to provide for us. As the psalmist testifies, "I have been young, and now am old, yet I have not seen the righteous forsaken or his children begging for bread."[6]

What about pastors who have served for many years? Should the church do something for them?

Of course, we are taught to honour those who have served us: "Remember your leaders, those who spoke to you the word of God."[7] Pastors with long pastorates and especially founding pastors should be accorded the *emeritus* or similar status with all appropriate honours. When I stepped down from my position as the first home-grown pastor, the church retained me in an advisory position and kept me posted on church matters through minutes of all board meetings. I was invited to speak on special occasions where there was always a warm welcome.

A church I know retired their pastor but continued to pay him salary for several years until he could draw upon his retirement benefits from the state. Such thoughtful consideration expedited the transition in that church. Not all churches may have that breadth of generosity or the financial capacity. But they should at least ensure that the basic needs of long-serving pastors are met when they step down.

Should pastors therefore expect such provisions from their churches?

They may expect but they should not demand. Like the Levites, those of us who serve in the vocational Christian ministry should look to God as our inheritance: "You shall have no inheritance in their land, neither shall you have any portion among them. I am your portion and your inheritance among the people of Israel."[8] This is not to say we cannot own land or house, but it does mean we should look to God, not to man or to the church, as our Provider. If I sit on a church board as a lay person, I would ensure that the pastor is well provided for. But if I serve as a pastor, I would not demand that the board provide for me. If I have taught the people well, and if I have served them well, they would know what to do.

Understandably, after years of service as a pastor, we often feel entitled to certain privileges and honours. Knowingly or unknowingly, we expect and demand them. About a year after I left my position at my church, I returned for a visit. I had been away in another part of the world, and the church had moved on without me. I was invited to preach at another church on Sunday, and could visit my former church only at their mid-week prayer meeting. So I sent word to the church that those who wish to meet me could do so there.

When I arrived that evening, those present were surprised to see me; no one had been informed of my visit. I was disappointed and wrote a note to the leaders wondering what happened. I will never forget what a deacon wrote in response. He made a point which hit the nail on the head, something to this effect: "You expected to be honoured but honour that is asked for is not honour. True honour is never asked for; it is given." I learned an important lesson through that experience.

So you are saying that while the church or the organisation should honour the outgoing leader, the leader himself should not have any such expectation?

Yes, if our church or organisation chooses to honour us, we consider it a bonus. If not, we wait on the Lord for him to honour us on the other side of eternity. Likewise, any church or organisation which fails to honour God's servants will have to answer before God on the other side too. Ultimately, we ask nothing and do nothing for ourselves but for the Lord.

EXPERIENCE OF SUCCESSION

You dedicated your book to four persons. Two of them are your predecessors and two of them your successors. How has your experience been with them?

My experience with them has been mostly positive. It can be seen by their willingness to have their names mentioned in my book. Two live in Singapore, one in Australia and another in Argentina. We continue to keep in touch, and remain as colleagues and friends.

What do you think you did right as predecessor, and as successor?

As predecessor, I had the privilege of working with my successors before they took over from me. Daniel was my associate for five years before I stepped down. Aldo was already a faculty member with the Institute when I started as Director of Training. With each of them, I forged a relationship of mutual respect which helped us through the succession process.

It was the same when I was the successor. Both my predecessors were also my mentors. Richard recruited me for the Institute, and coached me for seven years when he retired and I succeeded him. Swee Hwa was my teacher in Bible College, recommended me for postgraduate studies, and supervised me in the early years of my pastoral ministry. Some 30 years later, I was invited to succeed him in a church he had planted.

Would you say that your prior relationships with your predecessors and successors made it easier for the successions to work?

Yes, the mentoring process, whether planned or unplanned, was a great help. We see this between Moses and Joshua, Elijah and Elisha,

Paul and Timothy. For succession to work, the relationship between the predecessor and the successor is crucial. Unless there is trust, respect and consideration between them, succession will fall apart.

What in your experience was the hardest part of each succession?

It is how we give input without intruding or decline input without offending. Let me elaborate. As a predecessor, I want to be helpful to my successor. I want to give him feedback, but should I do it only when asked or when I think it necessary? On occasions when I had heard negative comments, I had asked the critic to speak to my successor directly. I refuse to take sides with any critic, always affirming my successor and generally giving advice only when asked. I believe it is wise to maintain a respectful distance.

As a successor, I appreciate counsel from my predecessor, and would seek it from time to time. At the same time I want him to know that I am not him and may not do what he would do. I am fortunate to have predecessors who gave me that freedom without feeling offended. Yet I find that managing my own feelings and those of my successor or predecessor requires much sensitivity, maturity and tact.

What do you think your predecessors and your successors did right?

I will give a couple of examples. When I succeeded the pastor who was once my mentor, he was required to report to me as the senior pastor. He agreed to do so, and followed through with a remarkable spirit of humility befitting a man of God. It is not easy in our oriental culture for the older to report to the younger.

At our training centre, my successor also impressed me with his thoughtfulness. A major multi-million-dollar renovation project had begun while I was still the training director. My successor saw it to its completion. When we returned to use the spanking new facilities, he invited me to give the dedicatory prayer. He could have done it himself, and his gesture touched me deeply.

CULTURE AND SUCCESSION

You made reference to culture. How does the cultural factor help or hinder the succession process?

I struggle with cultural issues in matters of leadership and succession. In Asia and some other parts of the world, "saving face" means trying our utmost to preserve our public image, even to the point of projecting a false front. I sat in a meeting once when an elderly leader offered to step down from his position after many decades of service. Almost everyone in the room persuaded him to stay on. Yet a few of them had earlier confided with me that the leader's retirement should be respected. To confound the situation further, the retiring leader later expressed to me his unhappiness with a fellow-leader who did not ask him to stay on!

Such a cultural framework makes it difficult to discern the true intentions of a person: Does he or does he not want to step down? Do we or do we not want him to stay? I wonder if Jesus' injunction for us to let our *Yes* be *Yes* and our *No* be *No* should apply here.[9] Another cultural factor which I already mentioned concerns age. When I was Vice-President of International Training at Haggai Institute, the reporting line was such that the entire chain had the older reporting to the younger. The two who reported to me were older than I was, and the one I reported to was younger than I. Yet our relationships were marked by mutual respect, and age did not feature at all. In fact, such submission of the older to the younger seems to be a pattern in Scriptures, as seen in Jacob and Esau, Joseph and David and their brothers.

How should we handle such cultural norms, especially when they are so deeply seated?

We should subject culture to Scripture and do what Scripture teaches. For example, in Jesus' parable, for the father to run out to meet his prodigal would be culturally unacceptable and unthinkable in the Chinese context. (It explains why a Chinese painting of that scene had the son kneeling before the father *inside* the house.) Yet Jesus portrayed God as acting against culture.

I think of the elder statesman Menes Abdul Noor of Egypt, pastor of the largest evangelical church in the Middle East. He thought and acted counter-culturally when he decided to step down at the prime of his ministry. When asked about the model of leadership in his church, he says:

> "It is common knowledge that no single person can monopolize the Holy Spirit. We have to work together, confident that the Spirit uses every one of us according to the talent given to him. This comforts our hearts regarding one another. The junior shouldn't fear that the senior might get rid of him and the senior shouldn't be afraid that the junior will revolt against him. There must be mutual trust.

> "However, we might err if we don't specify the responsibilities of the juniors and seniors. Therefore, each should have a description of his responsibilities and be assured of his privileges and limitations. I wish our churches would resort to professional, administrative laymen to help define responsibilities and evade complaints about unclear specializations."[10]

Such enlightened thinking is much needed. Successions are more likely to succeed when we agree to act biblically rather than accommodate to cultural practices which are not biblical. If "saving face" means protecting and inflating egos or skirting issues to avoid hurting feelings, then we should choose to speak the truth but speak it in love.[11]

SUCCESION AND MENTORING

What would you say to those who are looking for a successor? Should there first be a mentoring process?

Yes, definitely. Every leader should have a "Timothy" or protégé whether or not he is thinking of stepping down. We never know when we would be called away—to another field of service, another country, or even home to the Lord. Unless we think we are indispensable, we should adopt the dress code of the Israelites on the Passover night: travelling clothes ready to move.[12] More than a mentoring process, we need a mentoring culture.

What is a mentoring culture?

It begins with every member of a team mentoring someone or being mentored by someone. I once led a staff of four. Each one did his or her work well. But wherever one of them went on leave, the remaining three were at a loss how to cover the duties of the missing member, especially in an emergency. We ended up calling the person on leave for information and instructions. I decided to pair the staff, one cross-training the other. Later, when our staff doubled in strength, every staff member was acquainted with the work of another, and anyone could go on leave without being disturbed. Over the years, the occasional resignations of staff had little effect on the work.

The situation I just described is strictly speaking not a mentoring situation. The staff members merely shared knowledge and skills with one another. Mentoring involves more than that. But sharing our work is a good beginning. Too many of us work in silos, with our space narrowly defined and jealously guarded. Spiritual leaders are often given to such territorial tendency because their ministry involves personal relationships, privacy and confidentiality. They feel they cannot share with anyone what they know and do.

Is this tendency why such leaders monopolise the work?

We see this in Moses. He is the classic example of the busy leader who works alone. In the early years of my ministry, I made the same mistake—not only me, but the staff who served with me. Each time we brought a staff on board, he or she took on the work that used to be done by the lay people in the church. No wonder, someone told me to stop hiring staff, because it was making the people lazy! I will never forget a story told by my friend Reginaldo Kruklis who has the distinction of planting 21 daughter churches during his 33 years of ministry in Brazil. He left the three mother churches in the hands of successors, each of whom served longer than he did.

He shared how he had just begun a new pastorate when one of the deacons dropped in to welcome him. "I am here to help you build our church," he said. "O no, you are not here to help me," Reginaldo corrected him, "I am here to help *you* build the church." A simple switch of pronouns but a profound biblical truth as expressed by Paul: Christ "gave the apostles, the prophets, the evangelists, the shepherds and teachers, to equip the saints for the work of the ministry, for the building up the body of Christ...."[13] The saints, or the ordinary church members, are to be equipped to do the work of the ministry.

I saw this illustrated in the latter years of my pastoral ministry when every staff member we hired resulted in more people being mobilised to serve in each ministry. One of our staff was organising a major event held outside the country when his wife was diagnosed with a serious illness. He took urgent leave while I went as planned to the event and saw it unfold without a hitch. He had built such a team around him that they could do the work with or without him.

Isn't that a frightening thought? He could become redundant and lose his job!

Precisely. I sometimes hear leaders talk about "working myself out of my job," but I am not sure how many of us are serious about it.

If my goal is to keep myself employed, I would make myself indispensable. But if my goal is to equip God's people to build God's kingdom, then I would want to multiply myself. I wouldn't worry about becoming redundant and losing my job. In any case, such people who work themselves out of a position are often sought after for greater responsibilities.

INSECURITY AND SUCCESSION

You wrote about leaders who build their ministry around their insecurity. How real is that in your own experience?

I first heard this point made by James Houston when he visited Singapore in early 1993. I had just given notice to my church that I would step down when my elected term ended in two years. With no idea what I would do after that, I felt rather foolish. *Why do I want to leave a ministry that is bearing much fruit and bringing such fulfilment?* As I was taking Houston in my car to a public meeting, I sought his counsel. He shared about how God led him to leave his career as a professor of geography in Oxford to start a school of theology in Vancouver. He thought the people who asked him had confused geography with theology, but when they persisted, he relented. Like Elisha who burnt his ploughing implements, Houston burnt all his lecture notes—there was no turning back.

In his public talk, he addressed pastors like me and cautioned us against weaving our ministry around our own insecurity. I felt the message was for me, and I decided that, no matter what happened, I would not allow my ministry to become the basis of my security. Two months later, I received an invitation to serve with Haggai Institute. I learned that God never asked us to open our hands to let go of something without giving us something in return.

To close the loop, almost two decades later, in a brief sabbatical at Regent College where Houston is the founding principal, my wife and I were invited to the Houstons' home for breakfast. We reflected on the passage of the years, and I recalled how he had described his move from Oxford to Vancouver as "an infinitely enriching experience"—on hindsight of my own journey, I could not but add a hearty *Amen!*

Insecurity makes a leader cling on to a position, especially when he is enjoying it. How can such insecurity be overcome?

I do not know how. But I do know that leaders are insecure when they take their eyes off Jesus and look elsewhere for affirmation and acceptance. I reckon it will take a lifetime to find security in the Lord and in him alone. I once attended a dinner held in honour of a well-known Christian leader on his 70th birthday. Throughout the evening, lavish accolades were heaped upon him. When it came for his turn to speak, he walked up to the podium, opened his Bible, and preached for 45 minutes without once making any reference to himself or the occasion.

The next day, when I met to congratulate him personally, I commented that he made no acknowledgement of all that was said about him. His reply was sharp and crisp: "At my age, neither praise nor criticism affects me." I hope I would be able to say the same when I reach his age.

Is that how we know when a leader is truly secure?

Perhaps—but it's really hard to tell. I know for now I am still affected by what I hear, be it praise or criticism. I take comfort in the confession of a highly revered veteran leader who once heard a lengthy introduction flattering him, and prayed, "Lord, please forgive this brother for praising man instead of you, and please forgive me for enjoying every bit of it."

Security may be akin to love—more about what we do than how we feel. I think of my friend Rodney Hui when he was handing his position to his successor, having served in Operation Mobilisation for 30 years. In a paper titled "Antidote for Transition," he stated the following:

> - I must give up the positional authority completely, and not hold on to any of it.
> - I determine to stay out of the way of my successor.
> - I determine to support my successor.
> - I determine to reserve my comments and criticisms.
> - I determine to have the attitude to allow my successor the freedom to adopt, adapt and/or improvise what works, and abolish what doesn't.[14]

Someone who could articulate these intentions and adhere to them would be a truly secure leader.

Finally, do you have a last word on writing life's next chapter?

Yes, and it is this: God is sovereign and he both rules and over-rules. Though I have written about what we should do and not do, we should not think that we are in control. We are not. God is. I have been in situations where, after all human planning and effort has been expended, the outcome is still uncertain. There are too many variables. Only God knows how these imponderables would turn out, and in our prayers, we acknowledge with humility and submission for his will to be done.

[1] Dale Buss, *Family Man: The Biography of Dr. James Dobson* (Tyndale House Publishers, 2005), pages 11-12, 21.

[2] Jean H. Wong, in a testimony read at Mother's Day dinner by *Women of Zion*, Zion Bishan Bible-Presbyterian Church, May 2010.

[3] David W. F. Wong. *Finishing Well* (Singapore, 2006), page 77.

[4] "An Evangelical Commitment to Simple Lifestyle" is found in John Stott (editor), *Making Christ Known: Historic Mission Documents from the Lausanne Movement, 1974-1989* (Eerdmans, 1996), pages 139-153.

[5] Laurence J. Peter & Raymond Hull, *The Peter Principle: Why Things Always Go Wrong* (Bantam Books, 1969).

[6] Ps 37.25.

[7] Heb 13.7.

[8] Num 18.20.

[9] Matt 5.37.

[10] A. Yacoub & R. R. Mirshak, *A Witness to the Light: Dialogues with Dr. Rev. Menes Abdul Noor* (Cairo, Egypt, 2000), pages 70-71.

[11] Eph 4.15.

[12] Ex 12.11: "with your belt fastened, your sandals on your feet, and your staff in your hand."

[13] Eph 4.11-12.

[14] Presented at the East Asia Pacific Leaders meeting on 20 March 2010.

OTHER BOOKS BY DAVID W. F. WONG

Journey Mercies:
Navigating the Path Between Naïveté and Cynicism

Love's Rough Journeys

Journeys Beyond the Comfort Zone

The Jade Bangle

The Koi Pond

The Missing Chopstick

Make Them Laugh, Help Them Learn (Volume 1)

Make Them Laugh, Help Them Learn (Volume 2)

Finishing Well: Closing Life's Significant Chapters

The Left Hand of God and Other Surprises

You may view these books at *www.owlnook.com*. To order, please call (65) 9171 3834, or write Finishing Well Ministries, Clementi Central Post Office, P O Box 219, Singapore 911208.

You may write to the author at owlnook@yahoo.com..sg.